LIFE OF A GIANT.

Jason N. Peters

Table of Contents.

Part One: Who?

Part Two. - relationshit.

Part Three. – Society

I don't know if I'll ever write another book again, so here is my dedication:

This book is dedicated to anyone who's ever felt like they have no voice.
This book is dedicated to the depressed.
This book is dedicated to the teachers that told me I was too stupid to go to college
and the teachers that told me that if I focused I could do anything.
This book is dedicated to the college towns all over America, filled with anxiety over
unfair loans, uncertain futures, and the beginning of an uphill battle to get by in this
world.

This book is dedicated to my mother Diane, who deserves better than my weird book
and won't appreciate how often I curse in this book. I love you Ma.

This book is dedicated to Young Jeezy, Lil Wayne, and Earl Sweatshirt.
This book is dedicated to Jon Stewart, George Carlin, Joe Rogan, Dave Chappelle, and
Eric Andre.
This book is dedicated my best friends, the supportive cast of characters whom I've
met through all walks of life.
This book is dedicated to North Philadelphia, a place with more character and life
than anywhere I've ever been.
This book is dedicated to Dom Zupito.

CHAPTER ONE.

Think what you want. This is a book without persuasive intent. There is no intended emotional reaction to the text that lies before you. As a matter of fact, I as the author am unsure of my own reaction to this book. There are many ideas and opinions presented that to some may be controversial. To that accord, I am not concerned about reactions, unless they are informed and thought out. Religion, politics, capitalism, socialism, nihilism, tradition, culture, mental illness, and dating are a few of the themes that are touched on. There are curse words in this book.

If you have not noticed, this is not Chapter One, this is an intro or a prologue. I simply named it Chapter One so that people would read it. Personally, I never read the intro, so I am holding readers to the same standards I hold myself to.

To be acquainted my name is Jason and I have written a book, this book to be specific. You'll learn about me as this book goes on. *Life of a Giant* is a collection of short essays, narrative, and poetry; meant to show a different perspective. It's a chance to see the world through a different lens, I guess my lens, but the purpose is to understand someone else's logic and understanding.

Personally, I put little value into the idea of structure, my biggest complaint is the overuse of simple structure for comfort in all aspects of human life. There is a disingenuous nature that lies in the makeup of accepted structures. Most structure and order reside to assure safety and comfort, but at what costs? The rationalization for all structures as efficient and unquestioned is the reason why all suburbs look the same, why everyday people follow routines, why we accept being exposed to 5,000 advertisements a day, and America inexplicably operates in a two-party system. Structure is often a facade.

Consider a sporting event, there is little benefit **to the individual** in standing and singing the National Anthem before a game, yet every time we do because the order of events is structured that way. Why? Why not in the middle of the game? Why not at the end? Why do we rise from our seats? Why not balance on one leg? Why sporting events? Why not before work? Why not at 1 pm every day? Why at all?

It certainly benefits a nationalist mindset, which in turn provides comfort to a bureaucracy attempting to control 323.1 million people, who have convinced businesses that America is a stable market to operate in. That's why the national anthem is held in such high regards, the national anthem really is just a song. But the context decides what it really means depending on who you are and where you are, your "**If's and When's.**"

If I sing the National Anthem alone in my car, there is no context, it means nothing. If it's playing alone in my car and I am seated wearing a hat, but not singing, it means nothing. Yet, if I remain seated wearing a hat and refuse to sing at a baseball game, it means something. Don't even get me started on other countries national anthems. The structure of events and physical entities serve purposes intrinsically; questioning structure is as fundamental as questioning context.

You can see this applied to politics, Americans put such a large focus on changing the pieces within the structure, but rarely alter the structure. In reality, the election of a President is not nearly as important as perceived, if the same lobbyists and special interest groups have their hands in the game as always. Lobbyist and criminal Paul Manafort had connections to both Hillary Clinton and Donald Trump, the people involved in and around Washington do not disappear when the torch is handed off from party to party. Lobbyists don't sell their houses and move out of Washington when party lines flip, **they rebrand**. The structure that breeds misinformation and corruption is more the problem, rather than the interchangeable /electable pieces.

This book is intentionally structured in an unorthodox manner so that pieces can be read individually and/or as a story. The mix of poetry and narrative is done mainly because it provides a flow that I find pleasing and mirrors how I think. Narratives if too long drag and can get stale and pedantic, but poetry gets old after a while, especially to someone like myself who does not particularly love reading poetry.

This book is meant to ease the minds of the like-minded, and to elicit thought in those who are not like-minded.

If you disagree, great.
If you agree, great.
None of that is the point.

I've been thinking about what it is I want to do with my life.
But nothing seems to be right.
Not with me, the sciences, or the world; nothing is what it seems like.

The seams of the fabric of society often lie to me.
Privacy, scarce.
A public unaware.
Where do I find solace in a place so unpolished?

I worry that solace and relief are cheap, useless fixations for a nation striving for comfort.
Our main concerns, are mostly to learn and burn calories. Little worry about a place to sleep or a mouth to feed.

We should be comfortable in the most humble of settings, I'm betting that you want more.

I'm sure, because it's in our nature. Just like the need for a savior or our outlandish behavior.
I'll be fine in due time, we all will be.

The temporary makeup of our days pays dividends, the bad stuff always ends.
Then something else begins.
Whether it be the beginning of an opportunity, puberty, or something else new to me.
The chance to end one thing and start another is always here.
Fear is the only thing in your way today.
Or any day to be completely candid.
Let's manage to forget the baggage and move on.
Onto something brand new.
Can you turn the page?

STREET ROAD.

"I've learned a lot more being wrong than I ever did being right." I blurted out then jokingly attributed the quote to Mark Twain. That capped off the end of a very strange conversation where I also admitted to Dom that I don't think I'll ever be happy. He replied "you will be" and then laughed as if he knows something that I don't. It's comforting, it made me realize that those are the little moments where I am happy. I revel in my stupid sadness, sometimes for such long periods that I lose track of my life.

These moments aren't stoic or unfamiliar to Dom and I, admittedly we've known each other for 20 or 21 of the 22 years we've both been alive. He is like a brother to me in the sense of how complicated our dynamic is, we keep each other in check. Extremely different and similar in a way that I am with my actual biological brother. I am more open than he is, but that's just the way I deal with my issues. I won't air any of his dirty laundry, although I'm sure he'd be fine with it. But Dom is the type of friend that everyone needs.

Someone who won't blindly agree with you, someone who will stir the pot in temporary ways, never really damaging anyone, **but damaging something.** Someone who's your friend and you can't quite point at why, but you would kill for him.

Dom and I used to work together, at Panera Bread, Wings to Go, and Pizza Hut; all three places within a 5-minute walk of one another along **a street so bland and commercialized the town named it Street Road.** Dom was fired from Panera Bread,

I was fired from Wings to Go, we both quit the walking hellscape that was the Pizza Hut on Street Road. I hated that Pizza Hut so much that I used to mix antibacterial hand soap and lemonade in a dine-in cup, then chug it, forcing myself to vomit, in turn forcing my boss to begrudgingly send me home.

During the age of the temporarily popular and much revered 6-second video app – "**Vine**," Dom and I used to make clips of ourselves destroying the Pizza Hut in hopes of us getting fired. A video of Dom stabbing the inventory of Sierra Mist two liters with a butcher's knife or a video of myself dumping pizza all over myself to the sounds of Papa Roach were common place.

These stories may make us seem like delinquents and by no stretch of the imagination am I saying that we weren't, but those memories stemmed from a strange rebellion in us. Sporadic and unplanned behavior, there was a level of spontaneity and righteousness behind simply misbehaving that came naturally and made perfect sense to both of us.

I felt wronged, I wasn't a good kid, but I felt like I was a good kid. I was a mediocre kid that grew up near and around bad kids. Down the block from where I grew up, there was an almost cartoonishly evil bully, I can barely convince myself he did half of the things I witnessed him do. His name was Dylan, and he was a piece of garbage. As a teenager he smeared dog shit all over my older brother's turquoise 1989 Pontiac Grand Am and more sickeningly; cut my best friend's trampoline in half and put long florescent light bulbs underneath the trampoline. Sick-sadistic shit. That trampoline stunt is attempted murder to some degree. Compared to that, I was a good kid.

Yet, I'm 17 working at Pizza Hut, making no money and being treated like trash by adults that fucked up their lives. It all felt unjust. I'll tell you when it became unjust. When I was told about the *Cigarette Lady* by my Manager at Pizza Hut. I had heard rumblings about the Cigarette Lady and chose to ignore the things I was hearing. But all of a sudden, my manager approaches me and two other employees and goes into detail:

"Does anyone know if the Cigarette Lady is a lady?" – **Manager**

"What do you mean?" – **Coworker 1**

"Who is the Cigarette Lady?" – **Me**

• • •

"I always hear about this shit, what is it?" – **Me**

"Well, the Cigarette Lady is a woman of the night. A prostitute." – **Coworker 1**

"She's a lady that lives near me in Bensalem, that if you give her one cigarette, she'll suck your dick." – **Manager**

"And you're not sure if she's a woman or not?" – **Me**

"I've just heard some rumors" – **Manager**

"You had to know that was a dude suckin' on your dick. Right?" – **Coworker 2**

"How would I know?" – **Manager**

"How do you even get like that? – **Me**

"Why one cigarette?" – **Me**

"That's just the way it goes. I didn't start it." – **Manager**

I then walked away.

I think about that interaction often; Dom and I will still talk about the Cigarette Lady and the economics and logistics of sucking dick for one cigarette in Bensalem. What horrifies me the most is that someone is willing to accept that existence. How does the Cigarette Lady live? Why is my manager going to the Cigarette Lady when he has a fiancé? How many of my coworkers have met the Cigarette Lady? And how did I ever get in a situation to even be present for conversations about the Cigarette Lady?

I was frustrated. This sort of conversation encouraged further behaviors that would never be acceptable otherwise but gave us a free pass to do anything we wanted.

That same manager calls Dom and me into the Pizza Hut Manager's Office, which is only a computer and a stool next to the emergency exit. There's not even a door; it's so *'not an office'* that I would often make fun of managers for how *'not-an-office'* the "managers office" was. Regardless, Dom and I are standing in the doorway behind the stool in front of the computer where the Manager who gets his dick sucked by the Cigarette Lady looks at us and says:

"Can you explain this?"

Then goes on to show Dom and I, a video of Dom and I taking out the trash.

Immediately I knew what we were about to see...

I struggle to pull a bag of garbage out of the can.

I noticeably yell for Dom's attention.

Then throw the entire trash can into a massive dumpster.

We both begin to visibly laugh on the security cameras.

Then we proceed to throw all of the trash cans into the dumpster.

Go inside.

Come back out.

Laugh.

Begin smashing dishes in the back of the Pizza Hut.

Laugh.

Finish smashing dishes in the back of Pizza Hut.

Then proceed back into the establishment very pleased with ourselves.

Dom and I both look stunned and have huge grins on our face; we say *"sorry."* The situation was never spoken of again.

There's something about shared misery that can bring people together; **I don't look back on any of those days poorly.** I would never wish them on anyone because they are not right for anyone. "I've learned more from being wrong than I have being right. – Mark Twain" – *Jason Peters.*

The Perfect Present.

From invincible to invisible.
I've been on both ends of the spectrum.
It takes instances to differentiate which I'll be in the upcoming seconds.
Seconds of bombarding thoughts on irrelevant social miscues.
Seconds of bombarding thoughts on political issues.
Always having second thoughts on how I even got here.
Friends who are not here.
I've done a lot here.

But in a few years' time, time will erase the canvas of my memories from a place I call home.
Just like how I will erase the label of home from the canvas in my memories.
Life, like everything else, is on a scale.

How present are you?
We delineate between how much we let the future affect us
And how much we let the past get to us.
We never ever just protect us.
We're reaching, but for what?
We don't have all the facts on either.
Can't change the past. Can't know the future.
Let me check my computer.
The present is the only fixed false reality we know, and we can't handle it.
We've created days and time to dismantle this.
It's all got names.
But you know it's all games.
It's our system to thrive in.
A place to put our lives in.

Everything is so private.
Life's scary, so we hide it.
We know our fate as a species and as an individual.
Death, it's unconditional.
So we can fear, hate, and die
or we can love, joke and thrive.
And every once and awhile cry.
Because there's no reason to be alive.

That's why you must accept the present
Try not to resent it.
Because it's rude to complain about a present.
It was given to you; maybe you didn't want.
But here you are.

1/1

The past, glorified.
The present scrutinized.
The future, unidentified.
Me, swept up between hate **and** pride.

That moment that just happened.
Not this moment, but the one a few moments ago.
Where did that moment go?
What makes the important moments feel so slow?

Think back to the moment in the poem when you read the word
"*and.*"

No not these "*ands*" or the "*and*" on the last line. But the "*and*"
on the fourth line.

You probably just looked.

How about all the times you used "And" to connect two things?
What feelings do these moments bring?
Do they feel like something or nothing?
What is nothing in comparison to something?

Feelings are something you feel, but what makes them real.
If you pinch me and I pinch me, was I not pinched both times?

But under the guise of pain, your pinch hurt worse than mine.
You come to find, that your mind decides, what pleasures and
pains.

So, this life of all things, it's mostly a game.
Learn what rewards, and learn what does not.

No one told me not to touch fire because fire is hot.
No one told me how to think a thought.

No one told me that heartbreak has to hurt.
No one told me the truth about my self-worth.

Life is a game; evolution sets the rules.
As humans, we're lucky we figured out tools.
Now we've got the luxury of acting like fools.

The game of life is your own mind playing red light, green light.
There has to be more, all of this doesn't seem right.
The green light is pleasure that releases in your brain.
The red light is the opposite, controlling negatives and pain.
We like what we like, because it's best for the species,
But I'm gonna beat these.

To me, the species is as valuable as the time that they live in,
But time is in a quandary over its own existence, and the values
of the world have remained pedantic and resistant,
to reality or admittance of their own existence.

So we watch narrative on narrative, with a focus on humans
but doesn't that, at times, just feel stupid?

You already understand humanity.
Look in a mirror.
Sink into your shoulders, and let go of the fear here.
You are looking at yourself, how can I make this clearer?
You're human and special, because right now you're one of one.
You're the only one doing what's being done.
Your perspective on life will never be matched.
Because it's your turn at the game, and move quick, it goes fast.
Every moment in the car alone,
Not looking at the road, playing on your phone
Know.

That you're the only one occupying that time and
place.

You've got your one in one quirks and your one in one face.
Your one in one ways of handling pain
Your one in one brain, but probably not a one in one name.

I don't need god, and I don't think god needs me either.
I don't need the earth, and I don't think the earth needs me
either.
I don't need money, and I don't think money needs me either.
I don't need the government, and I know that they don't need
me either.
I need my friends, and my friends need me.
I need my family and my family needs me.

Those ideals do not deceive me.
I know that in this monkey brain of mine,
relationships are highly valued over time.
It triggers the green light,
but that trait just seems right.

Altruism is the future if the species will prosper.
But these tricky humans will sneak and imposter.
False prophets will foster a change and some monster
will spread lies as time shows, we're lost here.

Live your one in one life,
Don't take it too serious.

Bring others in,
Open or mysterious.

Hear them out
And be kind.

You don't know
What you'll find.

In due time
Peace of mind,

Will be alive.

Home.

Home is where the heart is.
But my heart is on my sleeve, so,
technically I mean, my home is everywhere my team goes.
I know a bunch of useless shit,
like pain and getting used to it,
the words atop some crucifix.
It's foolishness.
The truth is this; I'm not used to this.
I covet all my ruthlessness,
that's what got me through to this.
I'm new to this.

I've got a lot of problems.
Sometimes they're way too much to handle.
So, I sit and sip some shit that came right out of a handle.
I set bad examples.

But I let the red rum flow.
I hope I'm not as crazy as I seem.
Just living in a nightmare where I can't achieve my dream.

BLUE SWEATER –
A SHORT STORY.

Life is different now; I've been wearing this blue sweater.

It's a big blue sweater, bland, normal, safe; I wear it atop a long-sleeved button-down because I have no coat.

This sweater is an Extra Large, but I'm only a large.
This is a small enough detail to aggravate me every time I see my reflection, but small enough that no one else notices.

I've worn this shitty sweater in four countries, America, England, Ireland, and the Netherlands.
It fit in America, everything fit in America, but just because it fits doesn't mean it's good.

I hated myself in that sweater; my smile fake, my face fat, my brain scattered, my mind was gone.

But it fit.

Now in Schipol Airport I reach for this sweater, to keep me warm as I fly to my new home. Passport and boarding pass ready, Jon Bellion and Bob Dylan fight for my attention as I sip hot chocolate. I've drunk two hot chocolates in the past twenty-four hours, essentially just because I have no coat and I'm cold. Although I must admit I was going to get a coffee, instead I got two hot chocolates.

I thought it would be weird for a grown man to drink a hot chocolate. These have been the first two hot chocolates I've had since I was a little kid.

What am I worried about?

It's more than okay to indulge in things that make me happy. Remember who I was, I'm always evolving.

Hot chocolate is fucking great, and no one else cares, so why should I?

6 months ago, I wore this sweater on my 21st birthday, my smile fake, my face fat, my brain scattered, my mind gone.

I don't recognize that man.
I am that man, yet, now my smile is real, my face chubby, brain still scattered, and my mind is being found.

On a Spanish Airplane, I sit in this blue sweater, 3 days closer to 22 than to 21.

I want to live altruistically.
I want to love.
I want to be comfortable.
I usually talk to people on the plane, not today though.
I'm getting better at being alone.
I crave attention.
I crave approval.
I crave relatability.

I want to make you happy, because then maybe just maybe, something will make me happy.

I'm cold. I've seen Theresa, Nick, Dom, Joe, Chris, and Tony pass away. I've watched the people I love struggle no matter how hard they pray. I've watched my parents cry. I've watched friends watch their parents die. So how do we survive?

Me. I've been in my own head my whole life. I'm used to the cold. *You just can't freeze, or else you'll die.* I almost froze at a four-way intersection. But now, I'm backpacking from London to Dublin to Amsterdam for 7 days in late-October, cold. No coat.

I'm at the point where I'm used to the cold.
I could've frozen in the suburbs.
I could've frozen in the Pocono Mountains.
I could've frozen in Philadelphia or London.
Luckily, for now, I've got this blue sweater.
I'm not that cold in my blue sweater.
I can live and smile, but only the extreme cold will make me freeze. I won't hide from the extreme cold because I've encountered it before and lived.

This big blue sweater keeps me warm.
I will get better.
I will feel loved.

Life of a giant.

I mean I'm not a fuck up, but I've fucked up.
I've made green eyes cry
and I've lied straight to my mother's face.
It doesn't take a lot to take me back to that place.
My line is thin and unclear because trial and error have broken me.
Years where no one spoke to me.
Years with no one close to me.
I found me,
but you don't always like what you find.
With time, I must admit I'm getting used to that fact.
This isn't all an act; I'm just uncomfortable with my natural progression.

Knowing that I ended up how I am and you ended up how you are,
does not click in my brain.
Friends of mine have passed away, and some will tomorrow.
The obvious sorrow following their deaths hasn't quite clicked,
and I know it will hit.
When I look at my kids.
17 with a shotgun sounds a lot worse.
Your son in a hearse.
Brains dispersed along the walls of a tree house that you built him.
That's where his own mind that you made killed him.
I've got other friends making millions.
Resilience isn't an option sometimes.

Yes, there is an epidemic, but can we just admit the problem is that usually life sucks.
I'm an optimist.
Because I understand supply and demand.
Look at the issues, the drugs, violence, and suicide.
Yet no one will scrutinize
The fact that we all listen to a story about a man crucified for aggravating the system.
We crave an escape.
The story isn't religion, that man isn't god.
This is a story about distrusting power and doing what you feel is right.
Die for what you believe in.
In my case it's freedom
Just because I was born here does not mean that these rules and this system decide how I live.
How I love.
Who I am or how I trust.

Power is an illusion.
Money has lost its backing.
I am the one that decides how I am acting.
I need reasons to believe,
not in god or the state but that myself and my fate,
up to this very date have a purpose.
Even if this is all nothing, we should all try to make the most of it.
I'm not nervous because when it comes to having baggage, I've got the most luggage.
But ask any traveler, most luggage is expendable,
4000 miles away from home and I need a friend that's dependable.
Not my favorite shirt or my sneakers.

I need my dad as a teacher.
I need to start over; I am not my belongings.
These symbols are useless.
I have a longing to be comfortable, but comfort stunts growth.
I know this because I've never been comfortable.
And I'm 12 foot tall at this point.
Comfort is unsettling; consistency bores me.
I want to have a smile on my face when I am forty,
not because I'm pretending my son is funny,
& not because I'll have a lot of money,
but because what's done is done, and I've accepted it.
I don't want to look back and regret the shit I never said and
miss the chances I was shown.

I have grown, growth can be dangerous.
I'll grow to be hated; it's a fact because it's what I'm made of
It's non-negotiable.
I'm not a fuck up, but I've fucked up.
I'll fuck up again too.
Maybe I'll make brown eyes cry and lie directly to my
daughter's face.

Fine Print.

I promise the fine print is more important,
I assure it.
I've aborted all sense of misery,
I've learned to live for me.
There is no such thing as infamy.
Anything that's infamous,
can shift and twist to bliss.
But this is not in anyone's power
it's time that decides the narrative of your existence see.

It's you and me.
Trapped in the idea of time,
that idea is what defines the lines and rules we live by.
The culture is fabricated, the countries are abstract.
There is no America, and that's that.
Tell me what is real.

We know the brain named itself, could the rest of existence be a
manifestation of our subconscious.
A bit much for a poem, it's obnoxious.
But if you see a drop of dew on a blade of grass as the sun rises,
recognize what your brain recognizes.
Ask "why did that catch my eye?"
There are some surprises.

Have you ever caught yourself in a lie &
the lie was to yourself about yourself
And nothing else.
With no purpose.
I've heard this.
You wouldn't be you in 1832.

You wouldn't be you in 1925.
Sure, you'd be alive, but there's no chance you'd arrive at all the conclusions you've derived.
I know I wouldn't, I'm not well read. My whole life I've been fed. Born 200 years ago I'd surely be dead.

Just try to be happy.

Definition.

Humans, the small ones get bigger.
The big ones die.
This cycle continues until they no longer thrive.
They distract and create.
Attempts to be great.
Some fail and then crash.
Some get riches and cash.
To most this is life,
for most but not me.
Because I am alive in 2017.
My thoughts are absurd, from a generation that's brand new.
Millions my age that know not what to do.
Chase the money or decide to follow your dreams.
Regardless, pretending that these aren't just schemes.
What is the purpose, and why am I here?
These are the things that most of us fear.
Someone define life, can a genius explain it.
Where the fuck are the great thinkers?
Why aren't they on the A-list?
No King, No Kennedy, Aristotle, or Einstein.
Just your favorite celebs lip syncing on prime time.

SUPERMAN.

You feel invincible to a point, only allowing the unknown to affect you. There's this glow of self-assurance that comes with the critical nature of mental illness. I know myself pretty damn well, not as well as I'd like to, I still surprise me from time to time if I'm being completely honest. My behavior is sporadic and unstable to most but rationalized and measured in my own head. My depression has caused me to evaluate every fabric of my life in a narcissistic, self-hating, over-evaluation that ultimately beckons the question your brain is constantly presenting of "Why aren't I good enough?"

You're overly critical and introspective, in a way that causes you to lose reality in a sense. You're never sure if you're mentally ill or just a bad person.

In grade school, I always wore hoodies to cover my arms because they were very skinny and I thought people thought they were ugly. In Middle School, I grew out long hair to hide acne, but also to hide a face I did not like. Then in high school, I found alcohol and my insecurities became more linked to who I am as a person and my personality.

Promptly transforming into the current insecurity about my weight and how I am perceived. I still have a hard time looking in the mirror.

Call it body dysmorphia or complete lunacy, but it's the truth of my life. I have no sense of self when it comes to how I look and what I am "supposed to" look like.

The idea seems so arbitrary, the rules of fashion and attraction are completely subjective and relative to taste, time, the economy, and where you live. When there are moral and logical reasoning attached to a subject, I understand and can form an opinion with no reservation. Things become difficult when the topics are completely arbitrary, rules of attraction, fashion, and preference towards art; I no longer stress or worry about these things.

Depression has side effects or coincidences that are never laid out or explained in a medical pamphlet. My entire life is a byproduct or side effect of depression; it's in my behavior, the way I think, how I perceive, the way I understand. The development of empathy is one of my favorite things about my depression. I try to understand and be present with everyone I come across because I know how detrimental a social interaction gone awry can be in the wrong place at the wrong time.

There's a provided swagger and bravado that come along with the misunderstood. That's why the public is fascinated with "the other," and now more than ever, people who suffer from mental illness are a massive part of "the other," catching more attention in the mainstream, becoming extensively misunderstood.

Depression becomes an integral part of your personality, fused with how you think and understand the world. You can see it in others when you speak to them, understand how others are feeling, and empathize with whom you have little to nothing in common. I struggle in empathizing with *those who have*; there's a chip on my shoulder and an inability to relate to people who "don't struggle." This is all based on my false perception of other people and how they live, in reality, everyone is struggling in their own way and for me to pretend I understand everyone is obnoxious. When I perceive that someone has an easy life or hasn't struggled, I struggle to understand them.

It's important to be aware of your biases, or else you never address them. For me, I have a bias towards rich people and their lack of perceived struggles. But in that context, I too have never struggled in comparison to the majority of the world's population. Anytime I judge someone else, I ask, "Why am I judging this person?" and get to the root of the issue I have with them or myself.

There's a relationship between my conscious mind and unconscious mind, but it is skewed both for and against me. Having a brain that isn't 100% on your team has its benefits, there is a critical analysis of my everyday life on high alert at all times. I see through bullshit, I'm good at creating bullshit, and I love encountering bullshit.

I can't be offended because I care about my opinion significantly more than I care about your opinion, yet my opinion of me is lower than most people can comprehend. **You can't kill what's already dead.** You can't get in my head because I already occupy that space. First, you have to insult me accurately, simply calling me a "pussy" or making fun of what I'm wearing will never work, those things are too arbitrary. Once an insult is accurate, it has to come from someone whose opinion on the subject I value. After that, it has to be an insult that matters to me, is true, and is worse than what I already think. I feel like a superhero, and that's just the beginning.

I have built a filter in my head of the things that I will allow to affect me.

There is nothing I am afraid of. Nothing on Earth. If you don't fear death, why would I waste my time in fearing anything else? We're all going to die unless science completely eradicates aging and the degeneration of cells. That being said, as someone who thinks about death every day, death is something I see as a graceful and mystic experience. I romanticize death, it seems to be the only true peace, you come into life crying and screaming, you and your mother beat red and physically exhausted, but you die quietly and peacefully.

The nature of death is mysterious and beautiful, truly the most misunderstood part of the living experience. We've attached baggage, war, religion, business, and etiquette to death; when in reality it is the one binding experience that all living things share. The after-death question of "what happens after you die" plagues humanity, but the question of "what is death?" is rarely answered because of how we perceive it.

Does death occur when your heart stops?
Does death occur when your brain stops?
Is death related to consciousness?
Is death related to the soul?
Is there a soul?
After your brain and heart stop functioning, what do we consider the still living cells and molecules in your body?
When is someone officially dead?

In my opinion, death comes with the irreversible loss of consciousness and the inability to self-sustain without extensive use of technology or devoid of ability to recover. If I don't know my name and cannot physically bring a spoon to my mouth, consider me dead and throw me in the goddamn trash.

Walking through life ambivalent to my own existence, persistent to show myself that I can go the distance. Lost between two factions of the same entity, I put myself to work and don't let apathy get the best of me.

I'm like a Depressed Superman, impervious to the things that bother the majority of others, but my Kryptonite is my mind and the way it makes me suffer. I understand addiction and suicide, the side of society that we all want to scrutinize. But sometimes my mind needs to hide, and a little marijuana makes the madness all subside. The idea that my life is out of my hands is lunacy, but it's the only thing that's true to me. The prospect of one day being able not to feel this way; I know that I can get there and I yearn for the day.

Depression is a conflict; suicide is not the solution. Depression is a story; suicide is not the conclusion. In reality, the way we study suicidality is a fallacy, made to look like more than it's actually cut out to be. Depressed Superman bulletproof and hollow. Trying to be a voice for those who suffer to try and follow.

Comfort in Conversation.

Always punctual.
Barely functional.
Never comfortable.

Comfort thwarts ambition.
Functioning with a condition.
Punctuating my existence.

Reality? I'll need a night cap to fight that.
Trying to fight back.
When in reality, I'm not fighting, just trying hard not to feel bad.

For most, I'm a phase.
An event or place, you pass through.
Some choose to ignore; others feel as if they have too.

Always punctual.
Unbelievably comfortable.

Comfort comes naturally.
It's how I function actually.

My days fly by; I wish they would slow down.
My life is just perfect, living in the right now.
If I could change one thing, I'd stop all the changing.
Can't we all just be happy, look how I'm maintaining.

I can't function, but I am.
I'm alive now, aren't I?
I just can't find comfort in the fact I want to die.

Each day is a blessing, built just for me I'm guessing!
I just can't find out what has everyone stressing.

Things could be worse; I know that I'll hold on.
Just hard to find strength and the focus to go on.
Tried everything, there's not much to grow on.

> **There's nothing I can't do.**
> **I'd hate to be you.**

I'd kill to be happy, spend a day in those shoes.
I don't know what I'd do. What does it even feel like?
Being happy is so strange to me, does it even count as real life?

> **This thing that you're chasing, what's this blame that you're**
> **placing?**
> **What is so wrong that there is this life that you're hating?**

It's not worth explaining.
It feels so degrading.
Imagine one day; your will just starts fading.

Like an insecure line,
there are days where I'm fine.
But my brain can't sustain those days over time.

> **I'm so sorry to hear that, I wish I could help.**
> **Have you tried getting so---**

Tried, I've tried it all, drugs prescription and self-medicated.
I'm 200lbs with ADHD, and I fucking stretched and meditated.
Every single time, I got better then it faded.

It's like I went to school, but never graduated.
To you, this shit must seem exaggerated.
But I've tried everything, all options exasperated.

> **I don't want to dismiss this, but**
> **One day you'll look back and see how foolish all of this is.**

That's the thing; I know the bad thoughts are dumb.
Say what you want.
But it feels like One Day never comes.

MENTAL EVOLUTION.

This is a controversial train of thought, but I would like to elaborate on the evolutionary grounds of mental illness, with a focus on depression. With limited credentials to do so, I'll plead my case.

When referencing cures or treatment for depression, chemical options and counseling are the primary routes taken. In 2016, my best friend and I worked on a system of logging and calculating the data relative to mood swings. My friend, Ronnie, struggles with his own baggage but does not experience mood swings. We kept data for 50 days in reference to manic or depressive behavior, using a scale of 1-14. One was the most depressive you have ever felt, fourteen was the most manic you felt, and 7 was completely neutral. Similar in design to the pH scale. I kept track of this data over the course of 50 days, writing down keywords and activities as well; to see if I could be honest and recognize trends.

Over time, the data became both more consistent and the range of numbers shortened. Meaning, at the beginning of the logging I was up and down from 14 to 1 to 3 to 10, extremely volatile mood swings. But over time, the mood swings became more manageable and reasonable. We presented this idea at the Temple University "What If Innovation Fair" and received a positive reaction and I continue to push its progression because I believe it could help people over time.

My theory for why this works focuses on how I view depression and mental illness; it's a disconnect between the subconscious and the conscious developed through time and evolution. I say this because the majority of the brain's function or malfunction serves a purpose and the brain can be very tricky. Similar to our longing to be accepted by a group, to love, to eat, and all of your other inhibitions that stem from the formation of man, I see depression as another brain trick that requires a repairing between the conscious and the subconscious.

I believe this for many reasons; therapists are typically insufferable. May god bless them for their work, but if a trained healthcare professional tells me to be positive one more time I'm going to kill someone. Then, of course, antidepressants; the argument for antidepressants is that they "work for some people" but define "working" please. It doesn't "work" if you get off of them and can't function. If you're only okay while on antidepressants, that's essentially the same, if not worse than self-medication. Why? Because a primary side-effect of antidepressants is suicide. How is a behavior a side-effect? That doesn't even make sense. Giving a suicide-inducing pill to the most suicide-prone demographic doesn't exactly seem like the most logical way to be handling things.

I did my research, my girlfriend at the time had suggested I try anti-depressants; while I was trying to kick the habit of self-medication (blacking out drunk constantly). I trusted her, a doctor had also recommended it; and I had no reason, not to it. My biggest objection was "admitting I'm crazy" which is my preferred terminology to the extremely ugly terminology of "Mentally Ill."

My hate for the term "mentally ill" stems from many things, when does anyone use any of those words or even their root words in a positive light?

Mental - Mentally
Ill - Illness

Growing up, mental was an insult, short for *mentally retarded*. Nothing positive is ever described as "mental." You're smart, not mentally gifted. Also, "ill" are we kidding? Ill is a word reserved for people who are bedridden and green faced; it implicates weakness and irreversibility. When you have a common cold, you're sick; when grandma is hospitalized with a failed kidney, she's ill. Alzheimer's Disease is a mental illness; depression is a train of thought or an alternative consciousness. I only want to be called ill if it's from Lil Wayne, because "motherfucker I'm Ill, not sick." (sorry.)

After contemplating heavily, I decided to go onto the prescribed anti-depressants. Admittedly, death is looming at all times, but other than for a week in high school and one very sad night in the Pocono Mountains, I would never describe myself as suicidal.

A few weeks into my treatment, Zoloft had me feeling like a new man, confident, not scared of anything, happy for the most part. My behavior was erratic; I was going on long drives alone, heavily sedated for no reason other than to do it. But at the moment, you do not perceive this behavior as erratic or even see the patterns. In the midst of a massive breakup with the same girlfriend that suggested I take anti-depressants, I was admittedly numb for that time period, in the midst of a situation in which I would normally be devastated. The thought process was that numb was better than sad.

As I was on one of my aforementioned long and pointless drives, I approached a four-way intersection going about 55 miles per hour, as I had a thought that felt to be not my own. It felt as if some insidious being in the back seat grabbed onto my shoulder with a cold and rigid hand and just whispered: *"do it, no one would fucking care."* As the light turned from green to yellow then yellow to red, I sped up in a what can only be described as a sober-blackout. I had accepted my fate without having a conscious thought. My shoulders tensed with the touch and I don't know if I closed my eyes, but I know I couldn't see in front of me. The light had been red for six or seven seconds, cars are turning and going through this busy intersection, and then I'm there. I felt a weightlessness, the almost euphoric feeling of letting go. At that moment my mind decided it was going to cease to exist, my face expressionless as tears stream down my cheeks. Tears that have developed and fallen faster than I have ever witnessed or experienced, I glide through the intersection unscathed.

Sobbing uncontrollably in a manner that I never have before, I pull over into a CVS parking lot, open the door and fall out of my car like a stack of bricks tumbling. I lay, crying, face on the asphalt out front of a CVS, pebbles on my lips in broad daylight on a weekday afternoon and blurt out "What the fuck was that." Called my ex-girlfriend, to just hear someone I knew would care; I get a cheesesteak and carry on with my life.

As I said, death is always looming, but that suicide attempt was not me. I'm more pragmatic than that. If I kill myself, it will be significantly more elaborate, and I certainly would not risk injuring another person doing it. From that day forward, I gave up on anti-depressant, doctors, or taking advice about mental illness from someone who has never been through it.

Books like "*The Selfish Gene*" and "*Conscious Robots*" dive deeper into the development of the brain and argue some pretty logical theories and ideas. *Conscious Robots* focuses on a lack of free will and the development of the brain through evolution. It argues that our drive and inhibition stem from the need for our DNA to survive. Therefore we rarely act in our self-interest, but rather in the interest of the survival of our genes.

The best example Paul Kwatz gives in *Conscious Robots* is sex. Objectively sex is extremely unsafe. But our brains made sex feel good because it maximizes the probability that your genes live on. So, if you die of something contracted through sex, but manage to pass on your seed; according to your genes, it's job well done. **We are a vessel, not the product; a delivery mechanism for the chemicals controlling us.** We are the post office, DNA is the package. We are not the point.

That being said, the theories behind evolutionary causes for depression vary, mine is simplistic and helps me sleep at night. The development of man is rapid, the rapid development of technology affects the human species in ways we can't understand. We like to pretend as a species that everything is known and safe, but in reality; we know very little. Over time, the major needs of a human being were finding food and shelter, this was a time where humans were not as in tune with themselves. Now I have everything I could possibly want, and that part of my brain is dormant. The worry, fear, anxiety, anger, and fury that came with the hunts of early man, are still within us; but our brains are adjusting.

Depression is a transitional process of evolution for the human brain in an attempt for the unconscious to communicate with the conscious mind in a more fluid and efficient manner. As technology booms occurred, we saw an information boom occur, but what is information? Where does literally every idea on the planet come from? A human mind. The progression of society mirrors the progression of the brain.

Information and ideas are seen as abstract, but these ideas and thoughts we have come from electric signals and chemicals in the brain. We can't hold an idea or physically see one until the brain translates it into the physical world. Ideas are a form of energy, not taken seriously by anyone; our lack of technology or ability to think outside of the box at this time will show. Ideas have had the power to revolutionize the world over and over again, as technology develops the science behind how ideas occur will be attainable, and that idea will spark another idea as the world keeps spinning. Progress is hard-wired into our DNA, ideas are the driving force behind progress, our brains are literally the most important thing on the planet, and there is so little that we know about them.

I don't claim that this is all fact, it's my deductions and what I believe. I saw an interesting graphic presented by physicist Michio Kaku, explaining how time-travel is possible through the creation of a black hole. The graphic showed a rectangle representative of time, folded with a circle going through it. That's how I like to imagine the conscious and unconscious relationship and what is happening to our still-developing brains. We are bending the rules of consciousness, slowly becoming more self-aware, that's the rectangle, and the black hole is representative of a stream line allowing communication to flow more freely.

Both the time travel theory and the evolution theory have their holes. Michio Kaku and the rest of humanity are curious as to whether or not a human being can physically travel through space-time through a wormhole, could a person survive that transition? My ideas on depression and evolution mirror the same quandary, can a being as self-aware as humans survive the transition long-term. Depression is as old as society, but the rapid growth of both the population on Earth and technology seems to have pushed this development in a further direction. That could explain why both depression and suicidality are more prevalent in developed nations. The evolutionary perspective analyzing depression if right, shows that no one is "ill" rather, different and developing.

I still really struggle with mirrors. My reflection causes a level of discomfort that is unmatched in my everyday life. It's one of the most frustrating things that I have to deal with; it's not that I simply don't like looking in a mirror or seeing my reflection, but I physically detest it. I get an uneasy feeling in my shoulder blades, my heart rate picks up, and my head begins to pound. The strangest thing is that it's not my decision. The feelings of grief faced by the mirror in my head, resemble the repulsion felt by an unpleasant taste or smell.

The problem is not that I think that I'm hideous, the problem is not that I objectively hate my face, as a matter of fact, I don't know what the problem is at all.

Blunt Tried Eyes.

Test my blunt tried eyes.
See if they pass your test.
See past me and mine.
See if I pass your test.

Shy away from contact.
Shy away from my contact.
We tend to shy away from eye contact.
So what're you focusing on?

Are the connections too vulnerable when you stare into my
blunt tried eyes?
They look this way because I've been trying to close them.
No amount of smoke can turn my mind away.
Not today.

I know them.

I look down at my feet, or nervously fidget my phone.
Like you're not someone I've known.

Prone to the same misnomers and false judgments.

That've plagued man since time was first thought up.
Brought up being told misinformation.
The disintegration of any forward progress.
Processed through my blunt tried eyes.
My blunt tired eyes retire behind lids that's been begging to be
closed.

As these chemicals numb the chemicals numbing me.
This is a canceling out, or more of a canceling in.
Where to begin?
I add to subtract; it's standard self-medication.
I'm the doctor and the patient.

Impatient and biased in all my findings.
Because in the doctor's office I'm lying.
Trying to pass for functional.
Trying to pass for comfortable.

Bluntly I'm tired.
I've tried.
My eyes don't need rest, I do.

Part 2.

Relationshit.

"The opposite of love is not hate, it's indifference.

The opposite of art is not ugliness, it's indifference.

The opposite of faith is not heresy, it's indifference.

And the opposite of life is not death, it's indifference."

Elie Wiesel

49

—

You popped into my mind today.
Reminding me of times from other days.
Not to say they were all fine.
Fine, they were all fine.
In a sense that we both are fine now.
Come to find we're both fine now, makes me realize we were fine the whole time.
At a loss for words, which is rare for me.
An uncomfortable and not subtle rarity.
Now I have to live with this,
I'll just hold onto it and sit with this.

—

Admitting,
that I'm not living I'm existing.
Doing what the world's permitting.
Keep persisting and insisting that there's something more to living.

Live for others.
Live for them.
There's better days that come ahead.
And if you're dead,
you will not see,
what those days will come to be.

Indifference at first sight – Meeting.

Looking at you it seems as if you have glass eyes
Not to chastise your appearance
I'm just saying that I don't see through you,
You are simply unseeable.
I don't know if this is my problem or yours,
but you can't see me and I can't see you.
I'm not happy that it's like that,
To be even more frank, I'm not happy at all.
And if no massive revelation takes place,
we should just save face
& part ways.

Not a word spoken and I know we have nothing in common.
You're too happy, I can see it.
I'm too hollow, and you'd never understand.
As much as you try to see it.
I'll only resist despite how conscious I am.
I need love, but I don't want it.
I know I don't deserve it, despite the fact I'm worth it.
I'm just too hung up on the fact that I'm not perfect.

Indifference at Second Sight - The Date.

Okay, we're here.

There's a lot to lie about. How I'm doing, what I'm doing, who I am, and my intentions; not to mention that any time we converse more than a third of the conversation is based around the idea we care about each other. We can stare at each other and wonder what the other is really thinking, blinking to display that we're the same, but really that's all we have in common.

Commonly enough I'll fall in love, just like everyone; I too will fall for the trick of love, because it's the best drug on the planet. Nothing makes you feel better than love, even when manufactured factor in the fact that when love is captured there is a noticeable before and after. I fall in love often, aware that it's fleeting and inconsistent, yet everyone is persistent that it's some consistent rolling feeling. Healing all wounds, that you take to the tomb, love is not that simple or concrete, I would argue that it's not real at all. But I feel it all the time.

Love is fluid and omnipresent, similar to a belief in God, a belief in love requires faith. Argue that love is a trick made by the brain to save our brains from indulging in constant plunder, I wonder what a truly loveless world would look like. Luckily that's not something I'm subjected to, but we're expected to pair off in groups and venture to a place where me and a current stranger put both of our lives in danger in the form of dating. Dating is mostly persuading the other party to either touch your genitals or to keep you on a pedestal.

The hypothetical is simple, **imagine you're single, out and about in an attempt to mingle.** You see a person you're interested in, but now there are rules you need to play by, as a guy, I can't just go up and say "hi" because the men that came before me were excessive, aggressive, and boring; she's been harassed by men that are forty. Surely, I'm not like them, but on my end, there's all this added pressure, I can't explain or prove that I'm better. In the end, myself and a creep desire the same end result, I'm just slightly more noble. But I end up with a number in my mobile phone, to take home and continue the project of a romantic prospect. Typing and deleting texts like the rough draft of an essay, she doesn't respond until the next day, it feels like the best day of my life to get a text that says:

"Hey! Sorry I didn't get back to you yesterday! I was really busy, me and a couple of friends went out to the city!"

Fair. But how do I make it seem like I care? We all act unaware that the person on the other side of the screen isn't mean but also likely doesn't give a fuck about what you actually have to say. We spend more than half of our day either on the phone or asleep, we aren't that interesting but here's the thing. **I don't love me, so I need company.** Someone to soften the edges and love my lack of affection. I'm a better guy than portrayed, I've saved myself and gotten help, and now am on a quest to acquire wealth. But did you read that text? Girl, give me something to work with, I'm not trying to be a jerk, but this shit just gets on my nerves. It's almost worse than being curved.

No one actually cares *"wyd"* they just want to either ruin whatever you have planned or stand to pretend that your night is of importance to them. Send me something interesting like if you're in your car and a song comes on, and you wonder who else is listening. We all have the same stations, playing the same variation of 40 songs; whose got this song on? We could talk about who you are, rather than have shallow conversation with a lack of information, get drunk and numb the unnerving sensation that weighs over this interaction at every fraction of a second.

This isn't even anxiety, in the middle of our date I wish you'd say goodbye to me. I'm sure you're great and all. But I'm not. You're really hot. For once, **that's not the point.**

I'm so fucked up that I don't even like love because Dove Soap has nine different trademarked quotes trying to emote how much I should love Dove soap. I work in marketing; I see how love is generated then reinforced and venerated by media and culture then relegated into products and behaviors.

Yes, love will be your savior, but could you buy this Yankee Candle too? What else are you going to do to impress women? You need that candle. You can't handle being the only thing presented to this girl. We're simply not good enough. To get a good man you need a purse, makeup, the outfit from online. I'm worried about my hairline and how far it will go in due time.

Nothing's authentic, so my mindset is hectic, I don't mean to project it over the dinner table, I've just never been able to keep to myself. **Why the fuck is the calamari covered in Asian chili sauce?** How much does this shit cost? Now I need to eat an appetizer I don't like and keep a smile on, don't want to be the type of guy that goes wild on a waiter. But if she weren't here, I'd be in third gear on a hustle towards the kitchen, bitchin' about the fish.

Now you're drunk off well liquor and white wine, and it's time to wrap up and head home. Fine. I'll kiss you at your door, but

I'm never entirely sure if I should go into your place. The look on your face implies explicit interest in taking it further, and you insist I come in with a subtle squeeze of my package sparking a massive erection. She confuses that for affection, **trust me it's not**. Like I said, you're hot. I'm just not into you, but you've invited me into you and what's a guy to do?

You kiss me and say something; I literally feel nothing. The fucked-up thing is, I'm pretty sure that's why you like me; it might be that you feel you owe me for a night out, or you were looking to turn the lights out and do exactly this. But I hope that you're not pissed if we don't talk much after this.

You're beautiful and nice, but for some reason, you're not enough. **No one is, it was selfish even to approach you.** I thought that you could help me, but it seems like nothing can. I am a product of my environment, and I wasn't made to last long, *is that wrong*? I'd love to be a happy guy in a collared shirt with a sense of worth. But if I have to pretend I'm that to talk to some democrat over some Thai food; then my move is going to be never to see you again.

From the moment I walked out of your place I knew I wasn't returning, let's just both stay on our journeys, because I won't allow you to hurt me. My guards up and it's staying there because the game of love just isn't fair. So, tell your friends I'm an asshole because I bought you a meal and told you how pretty you are, curse me out next time you see me at a bar, it'll matter just as little as if you told me you loved me. It's not my fault that you decided to fuck me.

Love lost.

I've fallen in love a few times, each time it almost killed me
Hopefully, the next one will be the last one, and I think it will
be.
I know love is temporary, but that's why it's so powerful.
Once you taste it, it almost seems palpable.

There is love lost.
You can fall out.
There shouldn't be love lost
I wish I didn't fall out.

It is better to have had and lost than never to have had at all.
If lies had height that one would be one hundred feet tall.
How could you know the pain love causes if you've never felt
it?
How could your heart ache from never feeling love?
I know because I've felt my heart break, a pain that forces you
to be tough.

The worst part about losing love is about forgetting the feeling.
There is no real healing.
Just painting over the layers to try to cover past mistakes
The toll that it takes
causes a heart to break.
Nothing is worse than love that's fake.
I've faked love because I wanted to feel something,
But I need that real something,
I'm at this point where I feel nothing.

I'm bleeding out with a straight face and a dagger in chest.
I'm Kurt Cobain with a bullet proof vest.

I'm a lost cause in the midst of a long pause that you refer to as being alive.
I just want to hide.

Maps.

We're a lot to look at, the valleys and rivers that cover our faces
and bodies.
If I don't make an expression or say a word, stare at my resting
face.
Read it, and you'll find nothing.
But with each smile and glance, we give hints to the brain.
To what causes your fear and your pain.

Look at my eyebrows strain as I glare.
But why am I looking over there?
Our blemishes, our actions, our speech, our tweets
are just what our brains and our bodies want others to see.
You can never tell me that I never struggled.
You've never felt my anger bubble.
All judgments are biased.
You cannot judge me or read me,
But with just a sentence, I can plant just one seedling
to change the entire way that you might perceive me.

Do we feel different?
What does it feel like to be you?
When you are at your best, what do you do?

I know me.
My shoulders feel heavy when times are hard, tight and taut.
It's not a feeling you're taught; it's always been a feeling I've
fought.
Because it is followed by an onslaught of bad thoughts.
But the light yet fiery nature,
that comes along with some playful behavior,
has at times been my savior when I was nowhere near pay dirt.

This demeanor is an accumulation of everything I've ever been
through.
Every place I've been too
Every class I had to sit through and wondered what did I get
into.
I got into my own head, now I want to get out.
How?

SOME PILLOW TALK.

We laid in bed and smiled at one another, an action that should be getting redundant. I wonder how long until she's sick of this. You like to remind me how long we've been together; I like to deflect attention away from that kind of stuff. You remind me of no one, that's the best part about who you are. I've never met someone like you; I can tell you've been through a lot, you seem stronger than the average twenty-something college student. Prudent in action, tied to my stupid inaction. I look for subtle reactions when we're in traffic, and I get the opportunity to say something off-putting.

I like that you don't like all my jokes, I hope it stays that way. I think I've got a lock on your sense of humor. We're both funny, so we hate Amy Schumer.

I turn to you and say "Allie", and then you respond "What?" and I say "I wasn't talking about you, I was trying to think of something that's not quite a street... an alley." You probably will never laugh at something little and stupid like that. But I know if I come barreling out of bed naked with my arms out, it'll catch you so off your guard that you'll laugh so hard that you'll physically run away.

I can't promise much will come of this, because of how I am and the nature of my inability to feel comfortable, my mental state is so poor that I never feel good enough to deserve you, the love you show, or anyone for that matter.

My mindset is foggy, lost between the types of realities I'd love to have. The option of starting a family always grabbed me, but the closer I get to the age of reproduction the more I shy away. The idea of starting a family is one that I've always held in high regards as a potential solution to **my** problems. The reality is setting in, that I don't want my children to feel like me. I'm clinically depressed and extremely empathetic, the natural attachment I feel towards my family and friends often tugs at my heartstrings in ways that aren't reciprocated. I get too attached, the idea of having a mentally ill child makes me violently anxious, I'd be broken. This isn't a fun existence, why would I do that to someone I'm biologically attached to? Especially for reasons as selfish as fixing my life.

It also feels like cheating to have a child; it's a biological Hail Mary for the miserable, similar to drug abuse and all the other reckless things people do. Yet, childbirth and starting a family is a completely respected and applauded practice throughout human culture, despite being extremely difficult and dangerous.

There is a cost to the norm; it goes unrecognized because culture is such a strong duplicitous force. As liberal as you claim to be, or as progressive as you identify, there is always a judgment passed against those who abstain from "*the game.*" Those who "don't" rarely associate with those who "do." Very similar to how I prefer not to be around people who do cocaine, I also prefer not to be around married couples or vegans; they are the cultural other.

There's an added friction to our every interaction, some practices like cigarette smoking are not as culturally repugnant. A cigarette smoker can walk away, smoke, and return a little smellier and calmer than before. A cocaine user walks away, risks getting arrested wherever he goes to use cocaine and returns in an erratic and typically annoying state. But, the dynamics shift, if all of your friends begin to smoke cigarettes or do cocaine, you have decisions to make based off of the decisions that they have made. The dynamic of hanging out with five cigarette smokers or cocaine users, while alone as the only outsider are typically much different. These behaviors and decisions weigh over every conversation in the form of natural context.

Myself and a cocaine user cannot relate to topics dealing with reliability, finance, or responsibility without there being an illogical natural connection to their cocaine use. Cocaine is illogical, damaging, and costly; not to mention an extremely inefficient way to do drugs. So that decision carries over to their persona and context of their every action. Becoming a parent is extremely similar.

A parent and I, cannot relate to anything relating to reliability, finance, or responsibility without there being a natural disconnect directly caused by having a child. As a non-parent, you live and concern yourself with vastly different issues than a parent. Having a child is illogical in 2017 for many reasons, overpopulation, financial discourse/uncertainty, and the overall inability to predict the next decade. If you're a measured individual, with a standard life-path, high school educated, maybe college; shooting to make something of yourself, having a child is proven to slow your progression.

Having children because you feel as if "you should" or "it is time" is like the first time a teenager begins to drink alcohol, little rational thought into decision-making, very different outcomes. "Wanting" something is not a good reason to acquire something, contrary to popular belief.

It's the same societal pressure:
those around you begin to get involved, you consider, then feel the subconscious pressure of weighing the outcomes of each path, you make a decision.
Those who have children become friends with other people who have children, or attempt to hold onto the friends they have without children in a relationship that typically dwindles once the child is old enough to do basic arithmetic. There are outliers, but this distinction is not rare, it's basic in-group and out-group psychology.

"**Jason,**" she said, regaining my attention. "**What're you thinking about?**" I considered lying, knowing that I could be ruffling feathers by speaking my mind. I say something neutral "having a kid." She pauses, to say "I don't want kids." Surprised I respond "Why?" She says "It doesn't make any sense." Filled with a sense of pride and confusion, I kiss her.

We'd spoken in the past about our opinions on marriage, more or less calling it stupid and strange, myself calling it a farce to perpetuate reliance on religion and the state to reinforce monogamy to benefit an overall structure of society. I think the answer is somewhere in between. Planned tradition and ritual carry no weight to me; weddings seem disingenuous.

If a wedding and marriage are a symbol of expressing a couple's love, why would that be regulated and carried out the same way by everyone?

Wedding at a church, includes standard wedding ritual, big cake, DJ or band, chicken or fish, speeches pulled from Google read by people who can't deliver a speech, some rings, a week on a tropical island, and then back to real life. - Tuxedo and Wedding Dress.

But who is it for? We've all been to weddings before; we're seeing nothing new, just variations of the same thing. Is a wedding for the guests or the hosts? My argument is neither. **A wedding is for no one; it's just what's happening.** It's a lot of ritual and tradition, devoid of substance, and it's costly.

About a week later, Allie and I had talked about the hypocrisy of engagement rings. Diamonds are valueless entities; engagement rings are a symbol and symbols are useless. The issue I take with engagement rings is set in the same principles that make me hate weddings and marriage; **unnecessary organized tradition for the sake of tradition.**

If the idea is that an engagement ring is a "symbol of love," why is it always the same symbol? Why not a necklace? Blanket? Gift Card? Bowling Ball? Yoga Lesson? Or even nothing.

Shouldn't someone's expressed emotional support and ability to help you be enough? Nope. Three months' salary on a ring that will elicit joy for one week, primarily when a female gets to gloat to her friends about the ring. The ring is a symbol of socioeconomic status, nothing more. Standardizing love. Wouldn't it be better off to choose a "symbol of love" specific to character and personality?

I roll over, to face the wall, showing Allie my back only to feel a hug from around my back and a kiss on the side of my face. She knows I'm not in the best place and she's letting me be alone. I respect that, it means much more than a birthday gift or a sexual favor; because she didn't learn that from TV. That's the nature of a genuine interaction, you can feel it.

My disapproval of tradition and symbols come from a belief that tradition is a vehicle for comfort and normalcy, which thwarts innovation, typically in the name of safety and fear. You have a wedding to fit in; you drink the beer to fit in, you snort the cocaine to fit in, you pick your shirt to fit in because no one wants to be "out."

But the fact of the matter is that there is no in or out, it's all in your head. If I'm a single man wearing a Jesus Cross Necklace, an engagement ring, Buffalo Bills jersey, and khakis, it would be fair to assume that I am a Christian, with a fiancé, that likes the Buffalo Bills; all false. Not to mention the attributed meanings, to a jersey, cross, or ring.

Capitalism reinforces the idea that symbols are meaningful, intrinsically no symbol is important or valuable, a flag is cloth and a cross is wood. **To make me pretend, to provide others some manufactured level of security is not something I'm ready to participate in.**

Just because something means something to you, does not mean it matters to me. If someone didn't create the American flag, you'd never salute it. You don't bow to every lowercase "t" you see because it's a cross. The game of symbols and branding is a ploy used for grouping people together. You're supporting your team and buying objects, that's it. No symbol is reverent.

We lie in bed, wondering what the nature of this relationship is, both parties opposed to marriage, little interest in children, involved in a monogamous relationship, very much happy with one another. This must be the worry that fuels the want for marriage in people, it feels like there needs to be an added layer of security, eventually; but she and I revel in the unknown nature of our future, less stressed and worried because we were true in our ambitions.

Alumni.

I miss high school.
Things were so much easier then.
I know it's immature and I'm not supposed to because I've
grown so much.
But high school was the one place where things were safe.
My problems were so much easier in high school.
But that's just the past.
I've had to move on because I've grown too much for that.
I ran my course in those halls.
We had our nights, I felt like a king.
At times I felt invincible.
But to be honest.
Now I'm facing the facts that I'm not invincible.
And it's time for me to move onto bigger and better things.
It's scary; it's lonely.
I love high school.
But I'm not supposed to be in high school forever.

I miss her.
Things were so much easier then.
I know it's immature and I'm not supposed to because I've
grown so much.
But with her was the one place where things were safe.
My problems were so much easier with her.
But that's just the past.
I've had to move on because I've grown too much for that.
I ran my course in those halls.
We had our nights, I felt like a king.
At times I felt invincible.
But to be honest.
Now I'm facing the facts that I'm not invincible.

And it's time for me to move onto bigger and better things.
It's scary; it's lonely.
I loved her
But I'm not supposed to be with her forever.

No one wants to be the kid reliving high school, but it's harder
than we think to give up something we once loved.

Indifference at Third Sight - Break Up

Another text.
This one's about your job.
Another text.
This one's about your friend.
Another text.
This one's about your ex.
I wonder what will be next.

I lied a couple of times this week because I needed a break from
you.
I could never say that to your face or even admit it to myself,
but it's something I do.
Not to any fault of yours,
of course,
I suppose I'm just bored.

Another text.
Acknowledging my excuse, but asking what I'm doing next.
Another text.
Hinting sex.

Fine, come over. I'm out of excuses.
Let's do this.

The same courting behavior that I've already done with
someone else.
Or a few others.
This isn't unplanned and sporadic, we've been trained through
past experience.
Fucking Surprise me.
I'm the furthest thing from naive.

I'm trying to find the will to start trying.
So sick of lying.

But it's been longer than it should've been.
It's been better than it could've been.
But that's not what I'm shooting for.

Stop.
I couldn't live with myself if we do this again.
You are beautiful; it's nothing to do with looks, attraction, or
anything.
It's cliche, but truthfully, it's not you, it's me.
And I know that if you could see or feel what I see and feel.
You'd know that the cliche is real.

I stay stoic for composure and brace myself for my fear.
Causing someone else to produce tears.
I've been on both sides of this,
the last goodbye and kiss.
I'll dismiss you from my apartment like a prisoner finishing
time.
Fractured you walk, leaving a piece of you behind.
I'm hurt too, but I've just hurt you. So, there's nothing I can do.
Just sit and stew.

My depressive nature causes this behavior.
My manic nature will come hours later.
When I'm single for the first time, downing multiple bottles of
fine wine
Giving a vibe that I'm fine.
Goddamn, can I sell emotion.
But, if you zoom close in, you'll see.
Me.
The honest me.

My blunt tried eyes only know honesty.
And honestly, I'm not fond of me.

Not fond of this or how my life's going.
I'm single now; another girl asks me how my night's going.

Looking at her it seems as if she has glass eyes
Not to chastise her appearance
I'm just saying that I don't see through her,
She's simply unseeable.
I don't know if this is my problem or hers,

… it's my problem.
I did not cause them
But, I'm sure it's me.

So, let's just not talk, save us both the pain.
There's a lot to lie about.
And I don't have that in me.
My judgments are unjust because I don't even know you.
But I don't want to know you.

Indifference through Hindsight

I still don't feel rational.
The actual truth is hard to face sometimes.
In the distance, I see your outline.
What used to be mine.
A silhouette of regret, or more uncertainty.
You had hurt me.
But the scabs turned to brief marks that left these scars.
From words shouted at bars, cars turned around from a night
out.
I'm not about to reminisce and get myself to a frantic place.
I couldn't even see your face without feeling manic.

I was my worst self, knowing that is still inside me keeps me
honest.
I promise to keep those demons under lock and key.
Probably coming out in my weakest moments, I'll have to own
it.
The ugly truth is I am my flaws, and those components are
essential.
Mental state, dysfunctional. The sight of you uncomfortable.

I hope he treats you well, but you never love him.
I'm selfish and spiteful. I've never pretended.

If you kissed me, I'd be wary. I know those lips lie.
They told me they loved me.

Nothing.

My judgments are unjust because I don't even know you.
The lies come from both sides.

You trying to control me, me trying to control you.
See, no more resentment or anger.
I look at you like you're a stranger.
Mixed in with the crowd.
Loud, booming, consuming.

There's still love in between us, but I won't validate it.
There's still love in me, but I fucking hate it.
You can't hurt me because you've already killed me.
And I'd never trust your attempts to make me happy, no matter
how genuine.
I'll never let you in.

Now I stand, hollow. In a shirt you bought me.
Holding a coffee.
Knowing that if I've seen you, then you've already seen me.
No real thought in real time.
My body turns in the meantime.
Subconscious forcing me out the door, before I realize what I'm
doing, let alone the motives.
You notice.
Do I say hi?
Or just wave bye, claiming I'm in a rush.
Because if I see you blush
We might add another story to the saga.
Something neither of us are ready to do, but at least something I
think about, often.
Lost in a trance, I wave to realize **it's not you.**

Then I come too.

I'm persistent that I don't know about you.
I don't know what to do.
Between love and hate is indifference.

It's different.
It's vaguely vague, a state and stage of contempt **for** feelings.
Reeling for a heart or brain to be conclusive when nothing will
do it.
You feel stupid.
It lingers.
This is the hard part,
The heart part.

Part 3.

Society.

"Scratch any cynic and you'll find a disappointed idealist."

- **George Carlin**

THE RAMBLINGS OF AN INSANE CYNIC.

It's easy to get cynical. I ask that this book not be written off as the ramblings of an insane cynic. The definition of cynical:

believing that people are motivated by self-interest; distrustful of human sincerity or integrity

is not how the general public views cynicism. Cultural understanding does not do cynics any justice, making them out to seem like assholes with no positive views. Although these connections may be stereotypically accurate, it's immensely possible to be cynical without being an asshole. There are reasons to be cynical, because *"people are motivated by self-interest"* the proof is in the everyday life we live. We sleep for ourselves, work for ourselves, eat our favorite food, buy our favorite things, write our important thoughts, and think increasingly about ourselves. If your defense is that you have a job for your family, well you had a family for yourself; if your defense is that you had a family on accident, tough shit, you had sex for yourself. In our everyday lives, we are constantly *"distrustful of human sincerity or integrity"* because people are flawed, you need to be distrustful to keep yourself safe.

The slandering of cynics come from people who associate cynicism with the South Park depiction of it.

Stan Marsh sits in a hospital gown in his cardboard cut out doctor's office being diagnosed with "cynicism" after saying that both Tween Wave (a metaphor for Dubstep) and Bob Dylan "sound like shit." Many people watched that episode while conjuring up the image of someone cynical in their life. I sat in front of the television laughing because Bob Dylan and Dubstep both tend to sound like shit to me. Not to discredit "Like a Rolling Stone" or any of Bob Dylan's other very long tedious songs or the integrity of music made entirely of other songs (dubstep).

The problem with being a cynic stems from the primary issue;
cynics aren't cynical enough.

Cynics often operate under the false notion that "things used to be better" This falls under the myth of the "Good Old Days" a played-out trope that appears in comedy bits, Slate articles, and as filler in pretentious Communications textbooks. The Myth of the Good Old Days is the very obvious observation that the future is better than the past, things were not better when your parents were your age, things were not better in the 90's, the Renaissance, 1920's, and Biblical times were a nightmare.

History is written by the victor.

That's the primary reason for the improper nostalgia placed on time periods that we weren't alive to see. If we could hear accurate accounts of factory workers, farmers, failing artists, slaves, and the marginalized people of human history, we'd likely progress much quicker. Instead, we have accounts of the roaring 20's and images portrayed of the Great Gatsby. What about the people who cleaned up the parties in West Egg? Where's the story of the maid with a sick mother cleaning up Daisy's vomit the morning after a party at the Gatsby residence?

Who is the man responsible for changing the green light that Jay Gatsby cant stop looking at?

(I know the Great Gatsby is fiction, I just liked the idea.)

In a similar light, we remember the 90's as simpler times, rather than focus on the constant barrage of corruption, dissolution of the Soviet Union, and all the boring facts that people like to forget. We believe we are worse off with technologies because the relationship between our brains and technologies are in their infancy and we are adapting. To long for the days without technology is too long for the days where you were disconnected from everyone and increasingly susceptible to misinformation, disease, and violence. In 2017, it's hard to imagine that we'll look at these times favorably, but Donald Trump already has Democrats praising George W. Bush, meaning the turn around for nostalgia is roughly ten years.

Every second of the present is the best time to be alive, believe it or not, **that is my cynical view**.

It's easy to get cynical when you feel as if you've been lied to about major topics, but facts are facts. Most of us are at the bottom of the food chain until we choose not to be or are allowed to move up.

In the case of religion turning people cynical, it comes from a sense of being wronged. Being told a stern and rigid ideology and having it be presented as fact that controls your current life and eternal life, then coming to discover that it was essentially all made up. That can easily break someone down into pieces. The issue here is not malintent, a regular citizen like myself was told those lies by people who loved me, who also believed those lies. The issue is that as a one in one citizen the Pope doesn't know me, the Saints don't know me, and the God that I'm supposed to turn to is no longer a part of my life; but I know all of them, and they have wronged me.

You can't get mad at Santa for not existing. You can't get mad at others for believing in God. You just have to get over the fact that Santa doesn't exist and try to have a reason to smile next Christmas.

These same principles can be applied to politics or any other breaking point for cynicism, you were told one thing that shaped you as a person, but then you came to the realization that it's simply untrue. This can be done by many of the following things:

God
Religion
Music
Politics
Government
Sports
Movies

For me, I faced almost all of these, forced to become cynical in every facet of my life. I was told that God and the Government cared about me, Lil Wayne and Kid Cudi released Rock Albums, I lived through the lies about Weapons of Mass Destruction and the age of misinformation, I've been a Philadelphia Sports fan my entire life, and have been getting let down by movie sequels from the time I was seven years old.

Humans are to be distrusted, that's why we wear condoms, we're literally willing to let someone stick a dick inside of us without entirely trusting them. - *distrustful of human sincerity or integrity.*

Everything you do is scientifically linked to the survival of your genes. - *believing that people are motivated by self-interest*

In all seriousness, you saw widespread cynicism in music as people began to hate disco. You saw widespread cynicism in movies when Star Wars showed the world Jar Jar Binks. You see widespread cynicism essentially running American politics, Donald Trump watches Fox News and knows Alex Jones. You see widespread cynicism towards religion; people are afraid of Muslims and church attendance is declining in the midst of constant scandals.

These things occur from expectation, not reality. You feel as if you deserve the next great rock album, a stunning Star Wars saga, a God that loves you, and a government that isn't corrupt; and no one disagrees with the sentiment behind that. But, this is reality, expectations and sentiments are not as important as truth and action, and the truth is that you don't deserve anything.

You didn't deserve the good Star Wars; you don't deserve the bad Star Wars. You had absolutely nothing to do with the production of Star Wars; you didn't have anything to do with writing it, the finance, the technologies that went into making it, in my case, it was something that was around before I was even alive. The older something is, the more nuanced the ideas around it get. Personally, I don't care about Star Wars, because fiction that isn't based in reality is not for me, as comedian Natasha Leggero so eloquently put "I don't watch make' em-ups." But hearing people discuss the let down of the Star Wars prequels was glaringly familiar to my experience with God.

You're told your whole life that God loves you and cares about you, you're given rules, a book, community, and a place to meet. Then one day you watch a George Carlin special, and you feel a little weird, but you suppress that feeling and go to church on Sunday. In church you start to realize that you've heard these stories before, you know the structure of the mass, and it's like a ritual to you now; you wonder *"What's the point?"* You muster up the courage of months of contemplation to ask an adult that has bought into Catholicism their entire life, *"What's the point?"* only to be told not to question God.

Then a scandal occurs, a priest in the area is caught touching children, and as church attendance drops, people begin to transfer to public school, and even your family goes to church less. I ask my mother about the scandal, she cries, feeling misled and taken advantage of, likely wondering if her kids are safe and who can she trust. Ironically, she turns to God.

As their faith gets shaken, mine entirely disappears. I became what I like to refer to as a **"Cultural Christian."** I can walk the line of not alienating other Christians, I attend mass when it makes my loved ones happy, I see the value in some of the Bible and why it could be important, but I don't take anything literally, and I'm unsure about God. Most religions have their "cultural members" and actual participants, I'm just more qualified to refer back to Catholicism.

I begin to ask questions, use the internet, and transform from a Catholic to a Christian to an Agnostic to an Atheist to nothing. Atheism is a waste of time; it's like being a political Independent; it's a label that puts you into a box without any support, but has all these other meanings attached to it. Atheism gives religion a level of validity it doesn't deserve; I don't want to be called an atheist because it's a waste of time even to be talking about this stuff anymore. It's outdated methodology that so many people are stuck in because they won't rip the band-aid and give up on Adult Santa.

There's this strange narrative that comes up between Atheists, not to "ruin religion for other people" because it "helps people." The type of help that religion provides is a temporary comfort through lies and misinformation that has wasted the time and resources of the most successful species on the planet. We're dogs chasing our tails when we could be working on something that actually benefits us.

My disdain for religion comes from the time that we live in, the information in our faces prove that we can move from these false idols and false ideologies. Religion was extremely valuable and helped set up the foundation for modern society, but so was slavery to some people. The established laws and tenets of religion helped civilize the world, but also are responsible for millions of deaths. This isn't just about Christianity; this is about all religion, Islam, Christianity, and Judaism alike. The need for these structures are disappearing, and not unlike a business or a brand, they have to try and re-invent themselves. You see this through the Catholics new "Cool Pope" marketing campaign and the widespread division of Muslim messages of **A.)** we're regular people, please accept us **and B.)** join our caliphate.

The disintegration of the need for a God will occur over time, but unfortunately, I was born in 1995. Rather than being born into the godless world, I long for; I get to be a part of the movement towards reason and common sense, rather than ever see it. (if it ever happens) Shifts in religion, morality, and social movements take generations; but the internet will have a profound affect on religion over the next hundred years.

Cynicism comes from being let down, but don't simply lower your expectations, just think honestly about your actions and the world around you. Approach Star Wars knowing it very easily could suck, expect the Eagles to have a devastating injury, and remember that this beautiful disaster we live in doesn't owe you anything.

LAW & MORALS.

Life is not about following the rules as they are written. We all know this, but we never admit it. There's a type of vague respect attributed to rules, laws, and structure that are unearned and propped up on the basis of their unequal consequences. In reality, we rarely address the fact that in our day to day lives we provide leniency and flexibility to the rules and laws that govern our lives because human beings are empathetic and understanding of one another.

I've always struggled with authority figures. I see the entire idea of "authority figures" as invalid, the social structures that typically validate authority on a bureaucratic or personal level are usually tied to a social code of norms that is carried through culture. These stem from the following beliefs:

1. Culture does not validate stupidity.
2. Tradition, although important to learn from, is a construct relevant only in the present to appease those involved. There's nothing wrong with bad traditions ending.
3. Morals are relative.
4. People are multi-faceted.
5. Bureaucracy promotes dehumanization.

If morals are relative to time, then laws have the ability to be flawed if not updated. Laws are used to interest those involved in major bureaucracies. People involved in bureaucracies are not evil for being involved in a naturally corrupt system, they are multi-faceted human beings with their own story and lives.

The best representation of why not to trust law and rules are provided by time and history. It was illegal to speak about certain topics throughout the world under the guise of "God's rule" in the majority of the world throughout time. That's the reason "Freedom of Speech" is so widely coveted, the magnitude of free speech is often overlooked, there are many places throughout the world today that do not have the right to speak their minds.

Consider the logistics behind most laws and rules. **"Click it or ticket."** Seat belt laws made all over America from 1984-present day. The reason and logic behind the law seem to be obvious to the public "people should wear seat belts for safety reasons." This is a marketing ploy; this is how the government gains public support for a law. The public is convinced that the government is looking out for them and is promoting safety.

So, people can be pulled over and fined for not wearing a seatbelt in certain states. Giving the police another excuse to search people's cars and add fines onto other traffic violations. In Pennsylvania, seat belt laws are a "Secondary offense" meaning that you cannot be pulled over for not wearing a seat belt; it's only an additional fine.

What is the point of that? Who is that saving?

It's an additional source of income. That's all it is; the government needs money, so the government came up with another way to make money. It has very little to do with safety, but it's easy to get people on board for mandating a behavior that encourages safety. Mild forms of control add up. Certain people would say that a seat belt law is beneficial, but as I said, people are multi-faceted. There are groups of genuine, good people that want this law under the belief that mandating the use of seat belts will save lives and help people. There are also government employees in favor of the law because it means more money, more police jobs, more reasons to pull people over, and more power.

Admittedly, it's a strange to be this critical of seat belt law, but it seems a little less skeptical and crazy when you change the example from seat belt law to marijuana. Both draw parallels; marijuana laws are much less benign than seat belt laws. Both laws are perpetuated on the concept that it will help the public, both favor bureaucracy, and both have good people arguing on both sides.

The criminalization of marijuana has touched the lives of millions and millions of Americans through the years.

Okay, so why is marijuana illegal?

Admittedly, I have no idea what the rational justification for the demonetization of the drug in the year 2017 is, other than, "People are misinformed or evil." There are dozens of books and documentaries that detail the corrupt and absurd game of politics that led to the harsh laws involving marijuana.

These laws have in turn put millions of perfectly reasonable and morally acceptable people in prison for decades, typically racially motivated. (extremely racially motivated.) These laws halted the development of hemp products, which is used to make paper, textiles, and rope. Hemp made products are better for the environment in a sense that it produces four times as much paper per acre than trees and requires fewer chemicals. Hemp is also significantly more durable, renewable, non-toxic, and produces more biomass than any other plant that can be grown in the US. These laws also hindered any medical testing or medical use of marijuana, causing millions to get addicted to pain medication and suffer when they could have been in less pain. Demonizing weed could be blamed for sparking issues like drug addiction and not only allowing but provoking drug companies to grow into entities so large that they are too big to fail, translating to Fentanyl and the opioid crisis.

Yet, today people throughout America will be arrested for marijuana use. When my depression becomes crippling, and I cannot handle myself, THC is the only thing that can shake my brain up enough to get out of bed in the morning, we still barely know anything about these drugs, because it is still restricted in states.

Why? Because of people like William Randolph Hearst and Richard Nixon, along with the idiocy of racist policy, over policing, and the massive prison industrial complex. Money.

Culture and Tradition are at risk, the tradition of a massive prison industry propping up the American government and vice versa. The decriminalization of marijuana is coming slowly and steadily because the American Government has a hard time admitting it fucked up. Government is meant to feel infallible, releasing millions of people unjustly imprisoned for marijuana charges and repaying them for their time in prison is not something that they will do, even though it's the right thing to do. The tradition of marijuana being viewed as a criminal drug still stands for the majority of the population due to the intentional ineptitude of those in power. The anti-marijuana culture has prevailed throughout the years. In my experience, you should be wary of those claiming to "protect you" specifically if it's written into law, being sold to you, or coming from a huge company.

Morals are relative to time, information, and culture. Deciding what is just and morally acceptable to yourself is the only real guide to this life. This is not a perfect system because humans were not supposed to live in a perfect system. People are multi-faceted, some people find it acceptable to smoke marijuana, others find it acceptable to break up families and destroy lives for no reason other than money. We put one in chains, and we elect the other to public office. You tell me what is moral.

UTOPIA I

Utopia almost seems unfathomable. The dilemma of a Utopian society mirrors my experience with depression. You feel as if your depression is an extremely integral to who you are as a person. There's a process of progression needed that seems impossible and scary, but on the other side of that threshold are a new set of problems and solutions, predicaments in which you must now operate.

The idea of utopia is nice, but after all, it's an idea. As was society at one point, and in my opinion, the idea of society failed. We move cyclically through power structures, organized mass genocides, and the spread of plagues. The plague is now cancer, STDs, and obesity; the genocide is the refusal to feed and aid the third world in the name of capitalism (along with the actual ethnic cleansing of the Rohingya happening in Myanmar), and the power belongs in the hands of the wealthy (when wealth and finances remain the focal point of this society). Utopia is the halting of that process and living in perpetual bliss.

The steps towards utopia have been few and far between, communism although the thought of centuries ago has never been truly practiced, neither has capitalism. Pseudo-versions of these societal systems have been operating for centuries. In theory, American capitalism would be interesting to watch if it existed.

In America there is a combination of political connections to the private sector, tax code, and the way our political system dissuades socialism and promotes capitalism; so America sits on the fence in between the two systems standing up for capitalism and denouncing socialism while they strangely coexist. This causes a class struggle because the "middle class" is tapped for money by both systems; the poor benefit from socialism and the rich benefit from capitalism. The needs and wants are split straight down the middle in America because we have a media that perpetuates this problem without actually explaining it. Communism, when tried, amounted to astounding failure and famine; but I believe communism would thrive within a small, wealthy, and selfish nation.

"Are we closer to utopia or extinction?"

Extinction. As a species, we've worked towards extinction. That's why we've had nuclear weapons for over 60 years, but have done little to address world hunger or vast, widespread poverty. We've chosen the ability to blow up all existing life that we are aware of in the universe, over the ability to provide a meaningful life to those in need of necessities.

Maslow's hierarchy of needs always proves to provide a decent reference point for humanity. Maslow put together a pyramid of what humans need to live a fulfilled life. Although not specifically scientifically motivated, it's widely accepted because **it just makes sense.** The base for human life is set at the "basic needs" level, food, water, sleep, and sex included. Then stacked on top of that are "Safety" which is essentially having a secure environment. The needs following include relationships and friends, finishing off with belonging, esteem, and self-actualization. The two base factors, around the world, are not being met in massive populations in huge numbers. Starvation, intentional inhumane treatment, and insecure conditions ravage the world at alarming rates, the likes of which the world has always been accustomed too.

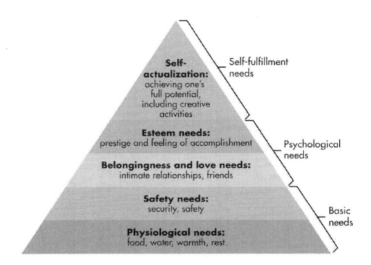

We live in a world of 3-D printers, sex trafficking, vaccines, super-viruses, mosquitoes, Doritos, the Super Bowl, and Ebola. Super poverty and super-wealth coexist, primarily in a relationship co-dependent on one another. I'm excited to see what happens the day Warren Buffett or Bill Gates dies, to see if they are real philanthropists or just shills that played the game the right way. Their mass wealth distributed correctly would be enough to take millions of people out of the darkness. This whole premise raises questions about all of the available governing systems. It seems like as a species we're all reaching for some vague sense of progress and forward movement, yet I was born into a world that already had sliced bread, and I don't know what sort of innovation I'm supposed to bring to the table.

This world we live in is overwhelming, there's an undertone of acceptance of completion and staying within constraints. I'm a grown man that has no idea how to make bread. Why? Because other people know how to make bread, that's delightful. I never have to worry about a yeast starter, cultured molecules, leaven, or other random words I've heard about bread baking. We see a car, comprised of parts, our phone, comprised of parts, we live in the age of ignorantly accepting finished products without fully understanding what they are and what they do.

The same stumbling over our two feet would occur in an attempt of achieving a utopia, but in reality, every day is an attempt at utopia, yet the world looks like a dystopian playground for those who **have** affecting those who **have not.**

In a perfect world, no one would have to preface. The messages being sent out would be graceful and informative. Advertisements would cease to exist because you'd be satisfied. Utopia is satisfaction and acceptance. But humans are not ever satisfied and refuse to accept anything. People walk the Earth for 70-80 years never swearing, never eating beef, or having sex because they refuse to accept truth beyond the lies that've been perpetuated for a few thousand years.

There's a need within humanity to understand, improve, and progress; the idea that this will halt at the creation of an Artificial Intelligence or medication that relieves my symptoms is ludicrous.

People don't understand humanity.
I don't understand my brain.
I can't even make a sandwich from scratch.

In searching for utopia, we will uncover darker issues and with more difficult consequences. In searching for happiness, I have uncovered a world full of darkness and difficult decisions to make. The second you think you have this world understood, is the second you recognize how stupid you are and how futile this all is. In search of utopia we've left civilizations in the dust and risk losing our humanity, but if we're the type of species that leaves entire civilizations in the dust, humanity is something worth wagering.

Repeat the Day.

You get out of your car and walk to the door.
You get out of your car and walk to the door.
You get out of your car and walk to the door.
How many times have I done this before?

Without a thought, alone and just being.
Am I even taking in the things that I'm seeing?

You take off your shoes and drop your keys in them.
You take off your shoes and drop your keys in them.
This is your life, and you simply repeat it.
We're repetitive creatures when I say creatures I mean it.

The weakest of primates, except for our brains.
But our brains are too strong, and we're going insane.

Walk up to the man, bow, eat the cracker.
Walk up to the man, bow, eat the cracker.
Walk up to the man, bow, eat the cracker.
Each time I do it, I let out some laughter.

We feel small often; there's no way to avoid it.
Let's just be sure not to let Jesus exploit it.

Hand over your heart, pledge your allegiance.
Hand over your heart, pledge your allegiance.
Hand over your heart, pledge your allegiance.
Read those words as an adult, how much do you believe it?

Your pledging loyalty to a land mass and controlling power.
Often times, doesn't that turn sour?

Live freely and openly, that's how it's supposed to be.
Love freely and openly, that's how it's supposed to be.
I'm just one man, and there's only so much hope in me.
I need to make sure I keep the good close to me.

Take away the money, what's there?
If you don't pay the state, they throw you in prison.
If you don't pay the church, you don't go to Heaven.
If you don't pay your friends, nothing will sway.
So, show love now, when else if not today?

Patriotism.

I'm so proud of my big feet.
They are the greatest feet on earth.
I tell each and every one I meet,
I've had these big feet since birth.

Respect my feet; they are important and grand.
Salute my feet, no matter where I stand.

All others are lesser,
Mine are much better.
That's why you and I should not be together.

My feet let me walk so much further than others,
Right now, I'm proud to be with my big footed brothers.

Others have small feet, no feet, and feet covered in sores.
But there's just one thing; those feet aren't yours.
They were born with those issues.
I was born with my graces.
I do not want those people in my sacred spaces.

I'll kill, and I'll fight.
Because that is my right.
As a man with big feet, I'll do that tonight.

Well... sometimes I wonder...

What would I do
If I had woken up and had no feet too.
Just like those people I see on the news
If one day I woke up and there just were no shoes.

Would I be helped or resilient?
Would I still be this brilliant?

The perks and the pleasure that come with my current
condition.
All come from dumb luck; no one made a decision.
My feet are glorious and strong, but I've done nothing to make
them.
And being pompous and rude will make others hate them.

Maybe one day, we'll all have big feet to be proud of.
But while others suffer, I'll keep my big mouth shut.
Use my big feet to help those that have none.
Because I'd rather have less so that others have some.

On bigfoot holidays, I'll remember those that never get to
celebrate.
Because they were born into something, they did not
perpetuate.
While refugees with small feet sneak and die in the sea trying to
flee,
I always keep in mind; those small feet could be me.

If I had money I'd help, I wish they knew I see them.
I wish that regardless of feet, we all just had freedom.

BREAKING: 24 Hour News Update.

Harambe and Cecil the Lion
A nation torn and crying.
There is no sensation,
the news media understands this great nation.
CNN, MSNBC, and Fox News focused on you; **unity and fighting separation.**
This is the best way to spread information.
I love this news and its very creation.

Everything the founding fathers envisioned
Bringing the most important stories right to your televis...

BREAKING NEWS: NFL PLAYERS KNEEL.

"This is a disgraceful act, that is disrespectful and wrong!"
How should I feel?
"They have the right to protest and kneel during that song!"
What of this is real?

Who is hurt when these athletes drop to their knee?
Physically? No one. From what I can see.
This issue is tricky; I don't want to conform.
I just need the news to help and inform.

But I see three news channels, with people screaming and yelling.
This isn't helping.
One channel says **"it's racist."**
One channel says "elitist."

Where are the facts? That's all I really needed.

Stop calling these channels **news,** that's not what they do.
They've got ad dollars and methodology to pursue.
It's not about you, and it's not about us.
They don't give a fuck.

If the money goes away, the news goes away.
That's just the reality of where we are today.
It pains me to say, but as of right now, we've seen the best that
we can get.
So, we try to put the pieces together on the internet.

But those people from the news get paid money for their tweets.
Because they knew that's how to get us in the seats.

I talk to friends about the issues, we all see things a little
different.
Yet, everyone on TV is on point and consistent.

Teleprompters roll, talking points recycled.
It's 24-hour news; it's a dirty, vicious cycle.

Dead animals you never knew, people kneeling during songs.
A Kardashian is pregnant, and that is what I saw.
Meanwhile, in Congress, their working to make laws.
That takes away our privacy and let banks grab us by our balls.

Distraction! Distraction! Reaction! Reaction!

All funded by the same people.
Claiming to be working for *the people.*
Seems a little bit evil.
But it's a charade that I see through.

Just because something's in the news or TV doesn't mean that it's important.
Fuck the NFL; refugees are fleeing Jordan.
Puerto Rico is underwater, and the nation is on fire.
But our system is corrupt, and the President is a liar.

People locked in cages for smoking weed, when it's sold as cancer medication.
The news runs stories that are best for circulation.
That's why there are no stories about the things that plague the nation.

Social Security not under scrutiny,
College Loans in hushed tones.
While we scream about emoji's through a fucking megaphone.

Television personalities covered in make-up, living their dreams.
Come onto the screen, with the fucking balls to tell me what to think.
They are all character actors in a live action play.
Living a lie that the world needs to throw away.

It's one big distraction to sell deodorant.
It takes some time to notice it.
But when you really focus it's not news, not even close to it.

Opinions tied to events and people used to push a narrative.

The more that you dig, the harder it is to manage this.
Political players own the media, funneling money into campaigns.
At the after-party, they sit together and pop champagne.

People focused on real change are demonized.
Very rarely is anyone truly criticized.
Everything Is Politicized.
EVERYTHING IS POLITICIZED.
And truth has been euthanized.

–

The Grey Party - a Numbers Game

323.1 million people
2 political parties

323.1 million people
2 options for President

Yet, nobody questions it.

323.1 million people
2 options that **nobody wanted**

323.1 million people
2 ways of thinking

These 2 parties must be really good.
These 2 ways of thinking must be very nuanced.

323.1 million people
4 Shrek movies
2 Puss in Boots spin-offs

323.1 million people
2 Bush Presidents
2 Clinton Nominations

This is the best we have in this nation?

One party is Pro-Life, Pro-Machine Gun, Anti-Taxes, but want
roads and hospitals.
Seems impossible.
One party raises taxes then pays themselves more, then wages
the same wars that they claimed to be against.

No matter your party, you're angry.
No matter your party, you're frustrated.
You see this every day and feel ignored in the things you have
to say.
There's nothing in the Constitution that says it has to be this
way.
And what use is a Constitution that allowed slavery anyway?

These parties follow trends and movements to stay in control
until they're old.

Hillary Clinton became pro-gay marriage in March 2013.
The Republican Party works directly with the Fox News
propaganda machine.
Neither care if Flint's water is clean.
But will throw you in jail for not giving them green.

I've been thinking of starting my own political party.
The Grey Party.
Its name and existence is an open admittance that these issues
are not black and white.

Belief in:

Real separation of church and state.
The abortion debate, use science to solve it.
A flat tax to be fair, a CEO pays the same percentage as that
man over there.
Guns, only in certain places, face it. We can never get rid of
guns, to think that we can is dumb.
Healthcare and welfare can be thought over once Citizens
United is overturned and citizens feel heard.

Businesses are not people.

For those unaware, the American government deemed that "Corporations are People." Evil. A plan that's so see through. They have more rights than we do, that's why banks are bailed out, and students just fail out. That's why companies default on their loans, and they get **our money.** But, if I default on my loans they can take my home. The rules are stacked against us. With restrictions that prevent us. Citizens United, fight it.

Lobbyists only make sense with structure and rules. But they've caused more problems and not solved them. Sugar companies lied, obesity rose, and people died. 2017 and people are in coal mines when we could fill middle America with huge wind turbines.

No paid leave.
Troops overseas.
They can send you and me if they see something they want to keep.
They'll say we're spreading democracy when we don't even have it here.
Then people's mothers and fathers will be in Iraq for 13 years. When they come back, they'll be ignored by DC and left with their medals and PTSD.
Homeless, underpaid, and ignored; when a recruiter in his 20's said that he'd be covered for sure.

The electoral college, but why?
In every reality, protect net neutrality.
FCC needs to adapt.
We've got WWE on TV, but then we demonized rap.
Refusal to acknowledge race relations.

Politicians are lying to their delegations.
America in denial never addressed its failings.
Now a reality star's the president, and DC is simply flailing.

I went to Europe; they think we're fucking crazy.
Met a couple of ladies that told me that they hate me.
Said I was a racist and asked me about my gun.
I explained that I'm not racist and that I do not have one.
And that was nothin.
When you leave this country, that's just the assumption.

Do you trust your government? If not, that's a problem.
We want politicians to be honest, but demand that they be
polished.
Smile and put on a suit, that's what you have to do.
Can't have an attitude or even be a little rude.
Well, that pissed off half the country, and now we've got the
opposite.
Now nothing's going to change, that's American politics.

The next president will either be a billionaire or a partisan hack.
Fact.
Because the people can never really act.

**Fuck a march, fuck a protest, fuck your movements, fuck it all.
The only way to make change is to get money involved.**

Not by spending, but carefully not spending.
Boycotts, of companies that undermine the people and be
careful of the message that you're sending.
Find the evil.

If all of America boycotted McDonald's for a day,
out of principle to show the government to listen to what we
have to say.
Just to show our power.
We'll stop electing "them."
Then instead of electing parties, we can nominate our friends.
I have friends that are smarter than the President.
An idea so unbelievable, I was hesitant to mention it.

The Grey Party, because the issues are rarely black and white
when there are 323.1 million people in the fight.

The Grey Party, admits that issues need to be thought about,
we shouldn't already have sides before we even know what we
are talking about.

The Grey Party, for now, something we'll have to dream about.

UTOPIA II.

To even fathom utopia, you must assume that it has to exist alone, must be inclusive, and be complete. Meaning that utopia cannot be "an option." In order to reach utopia, it has to be **"the option."** A Utopian society is devoid of resource inequality, which is essentially the reason for every major issue human's face. Utopia is inclusive and devoid of currency in a world or state of infinite resources or an absence of necessity of finite resources.

My little monkey brain can't wrap its head around the concept in any form other than a futuristic virtual reality and nourishment system. Very similar to science fiction texts, and Wall-E, that depict humans in chairs hooked up to extensive technology, with feeding tubes and chemicals coursing through their veins affecting their internal experience as their bodies are sustained. Even in this reality, utopia requires maintenance and updates, which means that it is not inclusive. The idea of utopia would have to be operated solely by a piece of technology that is safe, trusted, and has humanity's best interest in mind. Assuming that a place or technology exists, it would need to be governed by an omnipotent and "god-like" system of Artificial Intelligence, far after human beings are obsolete. The primary issue with the utopia via AI is the acknowledgment of another way of life; the human psyche would ponder what living outside of that realm would look like, driving people mad. That's not utopia. That's the point of the Matrix.

The only forms of utopia that exists are the brief and fleeting moments in which you are complacent and pleased. Utopia for some exists in the form of sleep, the only time they can truly be comfortable. The forms of utopia fantasized about are poorly constructed human mock-ups for the most difficult questions for humanity to answer:

"What could human beings accomplish if they were better?"
&
"What is better?"

The answer comes in time and changes while humanity grows. Some answers that have applied to our past have been:

cars, boats, electricity, computers, the internet, and more food

The other answers will be more evident in the future. The reality of the situation is that we're not the finished product. We're far from it. If humanity manages to stop poisoning its environment, killing and oppressing everything, focus their energy in productive ways and stop being so goddamn defensive about who owns what land and which land represents what; then maybe the nature of our beings and our situation will change, making a more reasonable version of utopia viable.

Some argue that socialism is utopia, to which I say what is socialism going to do about all of the people who don't believe in socialism, as well as racism, global starvation, and war. There are rebuttals to that claim, but the nature of humanity implies that those at the top of a socialist structure would become corrupt and jealousy would play its factor, as it always does.

Some argue that capitalism is utopia, to which I say, capitalism is intrinsically tied to evolution and anyone involved in a Darwinian-mindset should be extremely wary of the idea of utopia.

The choice to allude dystopia and further pretend that humans are some gracious being, above all others is a false narrative spoken to keep the structure in place.

There is no place in the world where <u>capitalism</u> in a true form is operated, yet it's been proven that <u>capitalism</u> if not managed properly can transform into a power structure used to funnel resources and power into the hands of a few. **Take that sentence and add communism, socialism, or a dictatorship instead of capitalism, it remains true.**

The issues that plague humanity do not come because the systems are flawed, they occur because people are flawed. The systems we choose to abide by are completely man-made and fluid, the second it begins to shift or change those in charge of the system alter the rules and functionality. Electoral College, Brexit, Health Care, War. The problem isn't found in systems.

The flaws that provide us with the dystopia we live in are provided by the way humans approach power structures when in reality the idea of power is an illusion perpetuated by the idea of economics and status. Utopia comes along with brutal honesty, the dissolving of ego and greed; and the development of empathy. The human mind is only capable of caring about a fixed amount of people, as our brains shift and develop, maybe this will change. But as we are, utopia is impossible.

SIX, 6, AND ANOTHER SIX.

6 things to be angry about.

1. That we pay the government's salary to control us, yet their behavior and lack of morals at the top level are worse than that of any workplace I've ever been a part of.

2. Trampoline basketball never really caught on.

3. When people from Texas, Arizona, and Alabama say they're "from the South." First off, Key West is America's Southern-most point. Second off, Texas is thousands of miles above the equator. You know who should have "Southern Pride?" No one. South is a direction; there's nothing to be proud of. You don't see me having "Northern Pride" because I'm from Pennsylvania or "Eastern Pride" unlike, Texas or Alabama, I live in the direction I claim, North. "Southern Pride" should be reserved for the people of Australia, Argentina, and Uruguay.

4. "Ignition (Remix)" by R. Kelly came out five years before the song titled "Ignition" by R. Kelly.

5. There is no commercial product available on the market that translates to low-cost, efficient, and simply made American Cheese sauce.

6. Golf, everything about Golf. It's a waste of land, time, and money. Incredibly expensive and elitist, bad for the environment, not exciting to watch, not fun to play (without alcohol), and doesn't help people get in shape. Golf is a multi-billion dollar industry built around fat old men dressed like idiots, poorly hitting a ball into a hole with strangers they don't like. It's a 70 Billion Dollar industry revolving around a shitty and inefficient game. If all of the top 5 athletes of major sports came together and had a battle royal, the golfers would be dead in 30 seconds. There is no value in a game of such little nuance and character. There is no value in a sport that is inaccessible to the general public. There is no value in a culture that hides away in country clubs. Imagine that golf didn't already exist, imagine how hard it would be to secure that amount of acreage for such a completely idiotic game. If you're not a PGA Golfer, but you spend thousands of dollars on golf every year, you're an idiot. Golf is a useless and infuriating sect of culture. Instead of playing golf, learn a language, build something, work out, or play a real sport. Shout out to Malcolm Gladwell.

Six things to be sad about.

1. French Fries inability to be effectively reheated.

2. The amount of time and money people spend attempting to make other people like them.

3. Your spouse is going to die, leaving you completely alone and old OR you are going to die, and your spouse is going to live on.

4. All of your favorite movies would be horrible without music. Not just the theme songs, the jazz in the background, the low hums and score in the Dark Knight, movies are nothing without music.

5. That no matter how sad you are, if you're holding this book, you're probably infinitely better off than the majority of the planet. But that fact doesn't help anything.

6. That the primary reason for your safety and lifestyle is the country in which you were born in, and billions of people never have a chance.

Six things to be happy about.

1. People continue to overcome hardship in amazing ways. The stories from rags to riches never stop coming. People worse than you have overcome.

2. The hardest days of human history are over. You don't have to worry about anything. Comfort is your biggest worry, most of life is getting out of your own way.

3. You can do pretty much anything you want in America if you're willing to waste $150.

4. One-day Donald Trump will not be the President.

5. If you have a house and that house has a basement, you can ignore the rest of the world and do anything you want.

6. All the questions you have about who you are and the life ahead of you will be answered.

Let it lie.

The truth tends to lie somewhere in the middle.
Lies tend to reside outside.
That's why we believe lies that seem to be benign.

We struggle with honesty.
Honestly, because if we were honest, we'd find how hopeless
we are.
Notice that the world you live in is simply a distraction and an
attempt to keep you inside the lines.

Find time to realize the things you don't realize.
The world around you was built for a specific outcome.
One we will never see.

We're on the tail end of life on this planet, in this universe too.
That, being said, only if science is true.
Because science is man-made too.
So when you ask me about how I feel, what the fuck am I
supposed to do?

Be careful who you listen too, what are their motives?
When they try to convince you, are they in your best interest,
notice.
Are they speaking to sell?
Speaking to tell?
Do they care if you're well?
How far have they fell?

Look for love in advice.
Acquire love in your life.
Because all of it could be gone in one night.

Whose love do you really feel?
And at that, what love is really real?

Stripped down to the basics.
How does one face it?
There's blame to go around, but no place to place it.

The truth lies somewhere in the middle.
Because the truth has lies sprinkled, just a little.
There's a lack of objective truth, that's just reality.
There are even holes in the truth of fatality.

We're so convinced that we know.
We don't.
Not even the basics.
Face it.

We live for love, without proof.
We accept death, but can't explain it.
We accept lies as truth.
Then inscribe it in the pavement.

I hate it.

We waste all our time and energy keeping the illusion alive.
When more than anything, we need this illusion to die.
Why?
I can't answer.
But there's a drive inside of me, and it grows like cancer.

PRECOGNITION.

The issues I have with science and our understanding of the
world comes from the arrogance that our universe is
representative of any sort of objective reality. Our universe is
"known" to be a small drop of water in an ocean, so what would
insist that our universe or perception of the universe is based on
any non-biased objective truth. If you subscribe to the belief that
there is a multiverse in which there are mathematically infinite
possibilities than this experience through time and space is just
one of an infinitesimal amount. Meaning that our "truths" and
"realities" are as objective as my opinion that the majority of the
people on this planet are mentally ill, and the people typically
described as mentally ill are just going through an evolutionary
stage of the brain that we won't comprehend until I'm long
gone.

There are theories that haven't been tested, realities unexplored.
Ideas and thoughts are responsible for almost all of the
advancements in human history since all anyone seems to care
about is human history. The creation of language forced us into
a new frontier of being able to express, explain, think, and
understand. But what allowed for the creation of language and
understanding? Where did the idea for language come from?
The understanding of precognition made me extremely
interested in the way I see the brain. Precognition is your brains
understanding of events and patterns, stored in your mind that
at times allows you to guess what is to come in the immediate

future before it happens. What a unique little trick to have picked up. Now I'm hooked on the brain and precognition, it's fascinating. Ever grab your phone right before it vibrates? Finish a joke you've never heard? Gotten upset before something bad happened? It's trippy.

That being said, ideas are the cornerstone of how everything came to be, yet no one ever talks about them. Have you ever had one of those freaky moments where you and a friend both say the same thing at the same time? Or your friend says the exact thing you were thinking but you've never thought before? People's bodies, breaths, and brains sync up after just 15 minutes of talking in something understood as behavioral synchrony. The worst thing you can do to a human being is to isolate them completely. Maybe there's a chance that we all need each other, and when we come together, ideas come to fruition that have never been thought of before. We don't entirely understand the nature and science of ideas themselves enough to have a new major scientific breakthrough.

There is shame seen in different ways of thinking, yet we are willing to allow people to take the story of Adam and Eve as fact. Author Chuck Klosterman highlights the extreme differences in how information is understood, disputing how gravity was interpreted throughout humanity's existence. In his book *"But What If We're Wrong?"* he explains that the way we in which we understand is constantly adapting, truths come to fruition over time. For hundreds of years it was believed that the Sun revolved around the Earth, now in 2017, we have the ability to make women's asses bigger and understand the shape and size of the universe. But do we truly understand anything? 1,000 years from now, how much of what we "know as truth" will be true? Look back 1,000 years and compare 2017 to 1017 then 1017 to 17; the manner in which our information is regarded will likely be seen as useless nonsense.

A.N.

It feels good to be well rested.
It's been awhile since I've been this tested.
For a few days, I needed to quit cold turkey.
Because the things that keep me sane hurt me.

"Show me what you're made of.
Give me something to be afraid of."

I speak, and then I repeat clearer.
Then I realize it's me in front of a mirror.

I can't stomach my own reflection too long.
My face disappoints, as a reminder of who I am.
Knowing that I am going to need to be strong.
Just to conquer who I am.

But there-there, nothing is fair.
And none of this matters, so why care?
Some call it pain, you call it a prison.
It's just the issue of Altruistic Nihilism.

Give it grief and criticism.
To me, it's the only true religion.
Not overwhelmed by euphemism.
Capitalism, skepticism, or narcissism.

No man in the sky,
Isn't that odd?
That all of this beauty could exist without god.

Every fear, every misstep,
Every kiss, every meal prep,

Every beer, every bite.
Every piss, every fight.

Less to do with Jesus, Abraham, or some religion.
But a lot to do with you and the sum of your decisions.
Mixed with a division between how we see the world we live in.
Seems a little easy just for all the credit to be given.

Today, my god is time; I need it to pass swiftly.
Because it's me versus myself and I don't want me to get me.

Trapped on an island as the grains of sand melt into the sea.

I'll let it all dissolve; then I'll let it take me.
Because much like myself, I know this island hates me.
That's why the island saves me.

Heels planted firm on a cliff, *the edge of sanity.*
Held in perfect balance by the subtle force of gravity.
I look down before me and see a pit of starving artists.
I peer behind my back to see the nightmare in the forest.

The forest thick with resources, but these forces seem morbid.
The forest plotted and known, understood and measured.
Up at the top, in the trees, are those who were clever.
Better.

That's how they see themselves, mainly because they feed
themselves.
Clean themselves, then have time to beat themselves.
They look down, and they enunciate clearer.
Just to let it known beneath them lives "bottom feeders."

Of the same genetic make-up, lost through wrong turns and
oppression.
Bottom feeders, are resourceful and need an outlet for
expression.
Mistreatment leads to regression, then succession.
Then war becomes the method.

Standing on the edge, how could I even question.
Teetering between these things brings anxiety and uncertainty.
I close my eyes and think of what this life is really worth to me.
I won't go into the forest, and I won't jump off the cliff.
So, I'll stay planted in this spot, my pants covered in shit.

If & When.

If it gets better, what would that even look like?
What is the longing for?
& how long until it gets old?
I've been told if I play by the rules and follow my heart, I'd be
fine.

It seems like **fine** is the height of satisfaction.

When did that happen?
If that's the best-case scenario, what am I even doing?

IF it gets better, how would I even know?
Where would I go?

It just goes to show how much we really don't know.

I'm affecting you somehow, that's the butterfly effect.
Except we don't accept this because we don't expect this.

Everyone you meet, see, hear and think about now occupies
some level of real estate in your mind.

Find time to recognize that face you've seen before, or choose to
ignore the people who come before you.

I'll try to reassure you that it's never simple.

Things seem like "*shit happened*" and that's how we're supposed
to see it, as natural.
But paths cross and lines blur. That's how you ended up here.
IF and When is the end all be all.

If you were born in Austria in 1932.
That's very much a different you.
You didn't pick you; you're a byproduct.
An accumulation of circumstances that somehow decreases or
enhances brain capacity and longevity.

Ideas, thoughts, and life's brevity.
That's why you can never get to me.
Because I didn't pick me and you didn't pick you.

This isn't my fault.
We're defaults.

One great great great great great great grandmother dies young,
and I never come into fruition.

I am a circumstance of decisions, a condition of - if and when
amplified.

If one person died and parents didn't multiply.
OR have sex at a different time, I wouldn't be alive.

Before we grasp life or the sun.
Can we talk about how we used to be cum?

We used to be smaller than that, single cells.
But what were we before the single cell?
Where was I before I had existed?
Where did I come from?

Why am I now?
How did this happen?
Who am I?

If my parents had sex at noon instead of eleven, who would
have happened?
Where would I be?
<u>**When would I be?**</u>
Would I be?

We are IF & When without if and when there is none.

So maybe life doesn't have to be fun.
Maybe I just have to do my part and be done.

I am if and when, by no means did I choose this, but I don't
know the "Ifs" so I might as well do this.

Eyes and Minds.

Eyes and minds lie.
Some eyes miss color,
Some minds want to fuck their mother.
So, if your mind and eyes lie at different times
Which is at fault.
If you can't see the errors of your ways,
The blame has to be placed
At one of those things that's inside my face.

I saw I was wrong but didn't understand,

Without my glasses, I couldn't see the man.

Why didn't your mind remind you to wear them this time?

Maybe, something dangerous is inside your mind.

Good choices are logical see they make sense
But a bad choice is absurd, absolute nonsense.

**The brain chooses what to do, how could it ever choose
wrong.
Must be from your eyes and the things that you saw.**

I made the bad choice of being a dick.
Because of some shit, I saw as a kid.

So, my eyes they picked up some poor sights, they're to blame.
For the times that I've had to deal with such shame.

Eyes and Minds,
In order to fix

The two must assist.
See the whole picture,
For just what it is.
These people you meet, they are just like you.
They care about their hair and the things that they do.

They've got minds and eyes, just like you.
And you'll never know them because you'll never know you.

Do you like the luge?
What's your thoughts on the mountains of Andorra?
I've never seen the luge.
I've never been to Europe.

What do you believe in?
What are you going to be doing 20 years from now?
Not as easy as favorite season.
So, you know yourself, but how?
You know what you used to think, but you don't know what
you will think.
So, you can never really know yourself or anyone else.
What happens when you have a spark of genius?
Was that thought hidden inside you this whole time?
What is the truth about potential?
I'm going mental.

You are not the same person from 10 years ago.
We do the same things with fears, you know?
You drop them over time, over years you grow.

This is humanity; things are fluid.
Everyone you see.
That's a person with a heart, brain, mind, and eyes.
Every mind and eyes are just surprise after surprise.

BIG KIDS.

You watch adults turn from these infallible beings into average struggling humans as you get older. When you're three feet tall, your parents seem like giants walking around with missions to accomplish and problems to solve. This portrayal of confidence is extremely misleading until you find out how incompetent and human everyone is. We're all just big kids.

Those insecurities that you develop as a child, along with your experiences growing up stick with you as you age. The world of adulthood isn't far off from the distinctions of childhood. Growing up I saw all walks of life available to me at a young age, going to camps, switching schools, meeting as many people as I could; because even as a child I had developed the tendency to value an escape. My inconsistent childhood led to my discomfort in consistency.

Switching from school to school exposed me to people from all walks of life, admittedly some more favorable than others. Public school and private school both have their upsides and downsides. For example, in public school from grades 1-5, I never taught basic grammar and was behind in Catholic School in reference to grammar and English sentence structures. On my first day of sixth grade, students began "*diagramming sentences*" which is a confusing activity even now in my adulthood, but absolutely perplexing to a 6th grader that is completely unaware what a "preposition" or "past participle" are.

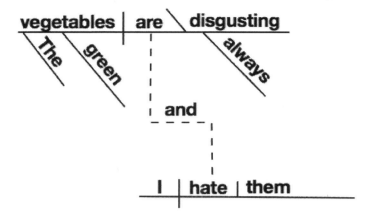

In private Catholic School, abstinence-only sex education was a prominent force. Teaching that you shouldn't have sex with a condom on, yet going on to kick out a pregnant student who had even decided to keep her baby. PRO-LIFE.

The issues I have with education are potentially biased because I was a horrible student. The class clown type, frustrated with school because of un-medicated ADHD furiously shaking me to my core. My teachers would reach out to my parents citing that I was a constant distraction in class, mostly because I could not focus on anything. Looking back at it, I was right to be distracting class; class was useless for the most part.

History/Social Studies Class:

In standard K-12 Education, you spend time focusing on American History, geography, and the intricacies of wars. The focus on American History helps build the pompous American psyche that views America as the center of the world, teaching mythology of George Washington, Christopher Columbus, and over glorifying the Founding Fathers; failing to show their humanities. Rather than going into the intricacies of the systems of governance and collapse of societies to learn from the past, we study names and dates.

Science Class:

The failure to teach the fluid and evolving nature of science affect the way that children who are interested in science view the field as a whole. The focus should be on teaching students to work outside of the box, while staying inside of the scientific method, rather than stressing that science textbooks are gospel when in reality, much of what you learn growing up gradually will become obsolete. This can be seen in how cell structure is taught, understanding the human body, and the way we approach teaching science.

Math Class:

I can't critique how I was taught math because I finessed my way through math. I never learned math, because calculators exist and I thought I'd never need it. Now I'm a college graduate; I still don't need it. Anything past percentages and long division is a waste of time.

English Class:

What help is diagramming a sentence if half the class can't spell "restaurant" or "definitely" when they are 22? The tendency to dismiss slang, not address dialects, and to not speak about the history of language or its effect on the species through time had never been addressed. Why the fuck are we still studying the

Canterbury Tales? None of my teachers even understood that book.

Religion Class:

Teaching incorrect things. Lying to promote an agenda. Basic fallacies and misunderstood texts.

College

I don't regret how I spent my time in class, and admittedly, higher education isn't better. I'd argue that higher education is worse. **I wish I didn't go to college.** The internet mixed with a genuine desire to be intelligent and a knack for curiosity is a far better driver towards becoming educated than traditional higher education. Spending tens of thousands of dollars for a middle-aged woman making $36,000 a year showing me a TED Talk on YouTube from 2012 or an adjunct professor, essentially paying to teach me, re-using a PowerPoint that a department head gave them. Education is held up on a pedestal because there's an assumption that it is done correctly.

After four years of college, having my name announced at graduation, and walking across the stage, Temple University called me back to their offices and demanded I take two more classes. I promptly enrolled in "Digital Mapping" a course in which I learn how to make maps, for no apparent reason. Then was also told to take "Intro to Graphic Design" which makes no sense, why would I be taking an Intro Class to graduate? It's a scam. Temple University weaseled another $5,000 out of another sucker because there are no other options.

Look at the two college towns I've lived in, East Stroudsburg University, which is surrounded by poverty and Section 8 housing in the Pocono Mountains; Temple University follows suit in the city. They take over low-income areas and slowly expand to drive people out, it's ingrained in the business model. Why do you think huge colleges are in the middle of nowhere? College is a business built on false hope, bad loans, and shady business practices under the guise of education.

The difference is, East Stroudsburg acts as a positive towards the community bringing in business and interacting with its rural surroundings. Temple University's interaction with North Philadelphia needs improvement. As someone who's worked 30+ hours a week for two years in a North Philadelphia bar, I see the lack of interaction with the community and the divisiveness that grows through carelessness.

It doesn't matter if it's mandated that frat boys need to clean up the streets once or twice a semester if those same frat boys are blasting "Jordan Belfort" at 3 am while your kids are trying to sleep. I'd hate to live in a college town at any age other than college age, yet there are thousands of us sharing the slums of North Philly. When someone who was born and raised in North Philly, feels oppressed and has little hope watches someone like me walk to class, knowing that I am renting their neighborhood to better my life, it hurts.

Median Household income in North Philadelphia is $17,696. A dean at Temple University makes more than $100,000.

Colleges claim to "provide futures" yet put their customers in horrendous positions. School spirit is a marketing scam, your favorite NCAA teams are exploited, and I'm supposed to say "Go Owls!" They have huge profit margins, massive influence, and are subsidized by our tax dollars.

Your alma mater does not care about you; they call you a week after you graduate for donations, after putting you in a crippling, anxiety-inducing debt. For some reason, universities are revered and respected "institutions" when in reality I flushed $100,000 down the toilet to receive a YouTube education. Massive businesses are not looking out for you.

This same sentiment of "looking up to adults" is pushed onto real life when you grow up, but you see businesses as infallible rather than adults. That's how colleges get away with it.

Cable down? Call your provider.
Something broken? Email someone.
Car accident? Call your insurance provider.
Call mommy and daddy.
Sit on hold, get store credit. There is so much shit to complain about; we literally have to employ people in other countries to listen to Americans complain.

Use fast-food chains as an example, when you go to a McDonald's you see a teenager at the counter, probably a toothless manager skulking in the background, and you're already anticipating that your order will be wrong. Now, if you're talking about McDonald's market share with your friends, you see McDonald's in a whole different perspective.

It's semiotics at its core. Semiotics can be defined as the study of interpretation. The terms used by "semiotics buffs" are signifier and signified; which is a little shoddy of communication specialists to name things that are packaged together so similarly.

Signifier - physical form, concrete, not abstract
Signified - the meaning or idea expressed, not concrete

Signifier - McDonald's Building
Signified - How you view McDonald's as a whole.

Semiotics breaks down the difference between reality and its attached meanings through society. In McDonald's case, it works to their favor, as it does for most corporations and bureaucracies. It prevents you from seeing a shitty ran down McDonald's as the image for McDonald's, the use of media, charity, advertisements, and news affects your image of companies every single day.

A Semiotic Review of McDonald's would look like this:

Signifier: Toothless Manager, Teen Workers, Cheap, Unhealthy

Signified: Family, America, Charity, Childhood, Nostalgia

These types of evaluations are why bad companies get viewed as larger than life; you can apply it to any major company. It's more difficult to do with individuals because individuals are real, controlled and measured all by one being.

Companies have the element of being comprised of multiple people and are able to create or compose an image through strategic planning. Then when human beings become a part of these companies, the facade is blown, and we all see that everywhere, everything is a shit show operated by huge children trying to be grown up.

The reality vs. the idea, that's all semiotics are.

The idea of who my mother is, against who my mother actually is. The idea of being an adult, against what being an adult actually is.

The fascinating parts of life we gloss over while fantasizing about the same shit that people have been fantasizing about for years drives me insane. Aren't we all sick of having the same thoughts? Aren't we all sick of being so predictable? In America we've standardized life, we all are expected to fit into these little holes, and to venture outside of those holes is seen as obscure.

The things that were supposed to make us freer, in turn, standardized what it means to be alive.

This is not to say that our lives are all exact replicas, but even at our most intimate, we can relate to the most random strangers. That's why media and advertisements work, I can speak of my experience with a toothless McDonald's manager, and despite none of you knowing that I'm talking about the 90's Sports Themed McDonald's on Street Road in Feasterville, Pennsylvania; **you understand.** This reality is the basis for communication. The ability to relate and empathize carries the species forward, but also can be taken advantage of.

It's seen as crazy not to want to relate, yet all of us want to be individuals. The contradictory nature of humanity is shown in this way; we want to be seen as individuals and accepted as part of a group.

My father is a genius, he'd hate me saying this, but he is. He has some Zen-like quality to him that I've only seen displayed in him. The type of man willing to commute four hours every day to put food on the table, the type of man who knows more about trains than the entire Amtrak company, and the type of man who can listen to novels in Morse Code while driving me to soccer. I am not sure if he ever meant to teach me this lesson, but over the years he constantly referred to life in the sense of a Bell Curve.

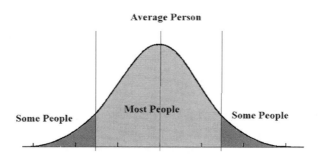

My father tends to repeat himself, a trait in which he has passed down to me.

So, the conversation can be remembered almost verbatim. I'd ask a question about almost anything, and my father would explain:

"Jason, do you know what a bell curve is?"

To which I'd respond, **"No"** because I'm forgetful and not the brightest.

"Well, grades to a test typically get graded and look something like a bell curve on a graph, like this." He says as he moves his finger up a slope and back down, waving a bell curve onto a grid in the air. *"Your smart kids on the one side, the idiots on the other side, and in the middle, lies the majority."*

"**Okay**" I'd say waiting for him to relate the two.

He would always ponder whatever "**X**" was and put it on a bell curve.

I use my father's methodology to apply to the things I just can't understand, mental illness, evil, sexuality, masculinity, or bazaar preferences. My father used this model to explain evil to me, citing that most people are not evil, but there is a small population that is evil and a small population of people who are morally astounding "Tim Tebow" types, in between lies the general population.

But the best way he ever explained it to me was when we were talking about idiots in the world. **Always astonished with the number of idiots who walk this planet**, my dad and I found the same intricacies of man exciting.

These kinds of conversations would come from someone taking too long to order their meal, driving poorly, or just seeing some schmuck at a 76ers game struggle to find their section. He said this to me:

"most people are smart within reason and can manage themselves on a day to day basis without impeding on other people. However, on the opposite sides of the Bell Curve are the geniuses, who tend not to be problematic (with exceptions) and the idiots, who tend to be louder than the majority."

I'm paraphrasing here but:

"The biggest issue with idiots Jason is that they don't know that they are idiots. They spend so much time being sure that they are right, that they can't even fathom the idea of being wrong."

Now that I am twenty-two and pretending to be an adult the same way everyone else is, I have to ask myself this one question: **"Am I an idiot?"**

My ideology is not rigid, and I see the world for what it is, confusing and difficult to understand.

I don't think I'll ever get a grasp of what this world truly "is." That's not to the fault of my ability, but rather a case of wrong place, wrong time. If and when. The mysteries of this world will be unlocked, far after I am dead. The rate at which the human brain is adapting to technology along with the development of knowledge and information progressing over the last one hundred years show an exponential trend that if continued will produce people far smarter than me with much more to work with.

Historically, I am not an idiot, the knowledge in my head surpasses that of most humans that have been alive centuries before me, even though I am by all means very mediocre in the present.

I am an idiot, if humans 5,000 years from now read this, it will likely be as primitive and nonsensical as cave paintings.

I think incorrectly often, obsess over things that are not worth obsessing over and have integrated technology I barely understand into my everyday life, seems stupid to me.

We as a species think we are smarter than we are, without understanding and taking into account the many intricacies of life.

We use languages without understanding why, while never accounting for what it has done to our once primal brains. Take pills when we don't know what they are comprised of. Use technology that we don't understand and indulge without understanding consequences. It's a privilege that came with time.

Explain how an iPhone works in entirety, tell me what's in Advil, and explain to me how you acquired your shirt.

We're all just big kids, trying to fall in love, have some fun, and not be bothered.

ORIGINAL SIN.

Excuse me, sir, if you don't mind could I have a moment of your time to talk about this upcoming presidential election?

I turn to the side and put my headphones in.

Excuse me, sir; I'm just trying to make change for the better.

I crumble up the pamphlet she hands me.

Why would you do that?

"In this juncture, I'm not prepared to deal with extra-curriculars including the following; passive aggression, asking me a question to provide some objection like *"why would you do that?"* as a passive suggestion to question my behavior.

I simply do not have enough time to sit and sign your petition to petition for someone you barely believe in, to grant whales freedom, or even diseases and children, to feed them. Because at this moment I'm focused on Susan G. Komen's bonus program. Don't doubt my sanity, because I doubt humanity. Pardon my vanity, but clarity is the only thing I have to provide, provided that there are replies sent back and then finally we can have a discussion on football concussions, fucking egg McMuffins, and the gender roles expressed in Doc McStuffins. But a baby born three years ago is yet to know what H2O tastes like in Flint, so I don't give a shit who your candidate is. The system is fixed.

With all due respect, I have to reject the invitation to sit back and neglect to effect the disrespect set towards the poor; I'm upset.

Not the poor like the few that abuse Welfare.
Not just the poor that can't afford Healthcare.
The poor that are stranded with no sign of help there.

The people with the same brains as us, not quite the same names as us, yet for some reason, there's no shame in us. With an iPhone running on stolen Coltan from the Congo, when those countries grow, revolutions will follow, remembering America as materialistic and shallow, that abused a continent with their economic power.

So, in essence, there's preference towards fortitude in attitude. This afternoon I'll ask of you:

'What is important?'

Jordan's, your mortgage, James Corden, the Lord, and employment? Join in on living for enjoyment. For some, that's a disjointed connection between joints and objections to the world's misconceptions. Actually, that's just me, for some reason that's how it has to be, see; I come from dumb luck. Stuck in this ever-growing chip on my shoulder, as I get older, I'm surprisingly not growing colder.

The opposite is happening. My father highlighted that everyone's liberal in their 20's and then conservative in their 40's. Surely, I understand the man's point. Liberal tendencies derive from the voices of the oppressed, stressed, and depressed. The conservative party, want to conserve what is best. But isn't that silly? The notion it kills me. I don't want to conserve the crime in North Philly. So, then we start building. But stop and wait there, proceed with hesitation; if you build too fast, that causes gentrification which leads to displacement and face it, the problems, who made them?

Those same people you hated before your empathy faded.

Being progressive in youth is an excuse, you saw the truth and learned there's nothing we can do. People quit, are complacent, as morons and racists take office, make changes that plague us, not now but when we're 40. Right when we flipped because now we've got kids and we're sick of this shit.

The guy in the red shirt means taxes are lesser.
The guy in the blue shirt is trying to pay professors, feed families, and make roads better.

I just can't claim that I am proud of America, humanity, capitalism, reality, or essentially anything.

This is a world where people like me get to be free, not because America is great. But because we are a part of a game, that a few centuries have made, and that America played especially well. These markets, movements, and institutions are abstract; fiction as a matter of fact. Yet, we forget about the real and much prefer the hyper-real, that lets us feel a faint simulation to trick ourselves into a brief sensation that used to occur from a hug or a vacation, your phone is hollow, will you follow its bright light?

The truth is this; I'm from America, I'm used to this. Cars, internet, freedom, and living as I please. This is able to happen because there are places in the world we allow to be ravaged by rape, war, and disease. Created by an economic siege on the rest of the planet. Three billion people live on less than $2.50 a day. So, say what you need to say, but you have NEVER had a bad day. Today 22,000 children will die from poverty. When in reality, poverty should be a novelty; compare life to Monopoly.

How does Monopoly money feel? Not real. Because it's paper. *Cash is processed with cotton.* But Monopoly money feels real as I build hotels on the boardwalk and watch as other players on the board walk right into the trap I placed. Just so they'd be hit before and after they pass "GO." I own all the property and now hold a monopoly on all of this board. Surely, you can see how this correlates as an orange man coordinates with the Grand Old Party, Trump owned a monopoly on the very same property, literally highlighted in the board game Monopoly.

So, Monopoly money is only real in the context of the game, how is cash not the same?

Who's really to blame for the sickening way of life we allow others to live in this game of life? It's you and me.

Born with an economic original sin of sorts. Born into a world of cotton candy and laser tag, as child soldiers my age eat rats and knit makeshift body bags.

Look at Laos, home to a thriving Ivory market because people's beliefs are so primitive they want animal carcasses. Trying to sustain on rugged terrain with no financial gain or global claim to fame. Laos citizens cry out because they have no rights and could be taken out for speaking on topics they know nothing about.

Well, every day we tell Laos to go fuck itself, we sit on
computers, playing first-person shooters, as a real first person is
something we've sutured into the world's culture through a
vulgar misunderstanding of the future. With reckless demand,
we command our will be done, but our wills are dumb. We
made a gun problem, created poverty, and every other medaly.

And none of that's the gross part; I feel like a blowhard trying to
become an artist, like Mozart in the face of all of this. I'd never
write again if I could build a civilization in need, feed those who
are hungry, and teach those lovely people what love means. Or
have them teach me, See.

Why not offer property to fight poverty? Offer vacant lots
stranded and abandoned to people willing to expand their
horizon to places provided that they build and help will a
community together. However they please. Unused land is a
waste of capital, can someone in this nation's capital make
actual change.

Yes! Gay people can get married, but there are mass graves of
people buried by illiterate soldiers, carrying guns with
American logos and nobody noticed.

They lie shoulder to shoulder; the soldier knows so little, they
did what they're told in a world without hope.
Too focused on a Taylor Swift song or whatever LaVarr Ball is
doing, is he ruining the game.

*It's a shame that his son won't play ball in the fall for a high school,
will he play AAU? That's important too!*

Because that helps sell shoes, which in turn boosts the economy,
probably creating jobs and paying taxes.

In practice no good happens, but we can pretend as pundits slant it; **America first, but then whose second? Or last? Typically, people who don't look like those men from our past.**

The founding fathers the slave raping authors referred to as "fathers." But ironically neglected their own daughters the same way they metaphorically did from not giving a shit about the mothers of their kids, by not giving them rights.

Like, we have to realize how time works. Everyone in the past was a piece of shit… not **everyone**, but even Gandhi had skeletons in his closet. Everywhere, murder in the name of prophets and exploitation for profits. We glorify the good and forget about the pain. We wear crosses around our neck and forget about the rape, the crusades, and the problems that were made through a message made by strangers from a different age.

Throughout history, religion was directly tied to the State, it was always about power, but people were uneducated. Now we're living in the future, these idols still venerated off of lies some people generated, motivated likely by the same ambitions you and I have.

They **wanted** food and water; now I **need** an iPad.

And that's my bad, I must confess, I'm not the best. It's the human condition, to improve your position, and go after your wishes, regardless of the situation that others live in.

I don't care about Laos; they were just a sample of misery and poverty in the world, for example, Syria is easier to explain because there's so much more weight in their name. Syrians are dying because markets have "nothing to gain" off their survival - we're still tribal. Treat religions like rivals, neglect those with skin tones that differ from our own pigment. Moldova is the poorest white country on the planet, and its GDP is 53,000 times larger than the GDP of Syria.

Okay, that was a trick, Syria has been taken over by terrorists, there's almost nothing left of it, life there has no benefit, and no one can rescue it; there GDP is ZERO.

These places are poor because they've constantly been exploited, no longer by slave trade; but by industry and low pay. Rich in minerals, land, supply, and demand; resources for phones, the power they don't know because development is slow because of the past that we know.

I'm no better than anyone, rather than joining the Peace Corps or helping those in need more; I consume the same resources that come from those people. Being selfish is a lifestyle; it's the capitalism we love, while we sit in self-made exile, with a big pile of Tostitos from a factory; food produced like textile manufacturing. Not for a second was I factoring in the fact that those methods of production could be reproduced elsewhere for smaller profit margins and it would stop human beings from starving. I just sit and eat my chips, in my apartment then walk on the tile, carpet and wood paneling. Handling my panicking.

Alone I lean my hand onto the wall just to feel if any of this is real. My last meal came pre-packaged, I got two for one on a deal.

A lack of concern causes terrorism when you mistreat people on purpose or unintentionally.

Imagine living in the Middle East, where fighting doesn't cease or Korea or Vietnam; or all the other places that we bomb. The lives ruined for you and your government to have a proxy war. We apparently voted for. I'd be mad too, of course.

Issues breeded by these people no one needed, America conceded just stole the things we needed. The hypocrisy of the need to spread democracy coming from a country ran by businesses and bureaucracy.

No, your votes don't matter but make sure you get out and do it. True, if a real candidate would emerge and I could trust a single word that they spoke, then know I'd vote. But for no reason other than control our options are limited at the polls to candidates that lobbyist know will do them favors later.

Monopolies run the country, actually rather bi-tri-opolies creating a new form of aristocracies, through buying and selling properties, influencing policies, and stock trade anomalies. Sysco, Monsanto, Google, and Facebook.

They worry about the debt ceiling, performing like they're really reeling knowing that if ever asked to pay up, it would certainly break up the precious markets, the economy, what they've been working hard and lobbying to keep intact, but it will never ever happen. It would pull out the very fabric of capitalism, but using basic actualism, we're too big to fail. Just like our president who should be in jail.

Enjoy your freedom and your toys, girls, and boys; but know that there's a cost. All of the lives lost. For a shirt bought from La Coste and Hugo Boss. From unjust wars, the slave trade, economic suppression, not to mention the oppression of women, people of color, people now considered brothers, sisters, fathers, mothers; that 100 years ago would have nothing. Something crazy about our species is that we never really get to see these truths of our past, I'd love to ask a regular person from anytime what they thought of their life. The human spirit is somehow strong in the face of all that's wrong. We have poetry, movies, and songs to make us feel we belong. It's amazing that we've made it as people, in the face of all the evil. Now there is the internet, a lens that we can see through. Peer into the war zone from your home. Talk to people in different time zones.

I think Utopia is impossible, at least with our Darwinian State of mind, the only chance at hope is empathy growing over time. A sense of care for the "people over there." Unaware of who you are, just like the people in their cars on the freeway you see each day and ignore. It's inconvenient to give a fuck, the world isn't all flowers, and a lot of people are intolerable; idiots are horrible. But empathy is learned, and sometimes it hurts when a friend takes their life, you're left by your wife, or you've had a bad night. But the fact of the matter is, that I'd rather be a clinically depressed, self-obsessed, erratic mess then have to put a bulletproof vest under my religious dress in an area of distress where people are chopping off heads.

BETA TEST GENERATION.

Without further adieu, I'll add my caveats. You need to be humble and know, that you are part of something special. Life. The years ahead of humanity are scary. There's a chance that we excel and dive deep into the amazing depths of our technological potential, there's a chance that technology grows too large to be contained and it leads to our demise, but there is also a chance that Moore's Law runs out leaving us to revel in the mediocrity of stagnant progression.

According to Investopedia "Moore's law refers to an observation made by Intel co-founder Gordon Moore in 1965. He noticed that the number of transistors per square inch on integrated circuits had doubled every year since their invention." This technological advancement is the difference between a Tamagotchi in 1997 and the Nintendo Switch in 2017. It's VHS to Netflix. Landline to iPhone. A 1996 Fiat Bravo to the Tesla 3. The basic idea is that technology grows in strength and shrinks in size at a steady rate.

There are many issues going forward in accordance with dealing with the inevitable end of Moore's Law. It will not be clear when it ends, which will likely prompt markets to hold up huge tech companies for years after their development slows, misleading consumers and leaving warehouses full, factories slowing down, and the market to become saturated with technology mediocre to the times. The public will be unaware for years that Moore's Law has ended and continue to buy products of little to no improvement, (similar to iPhone 7 to iPhone 8) then the tech bubble will burst hurting the ever so important economy.

I'm unsure when Moore's Law will end, I've seen scientists claim it already ended in 2016, there are predictions from 2020 to 2035 to 2050. Physicist Michio Kaku predicted that Moore's Law will run out in about 10 years, meaning that this lifestyle shift is one that humanity is going to very much have to adapt too.

From the time I was a child, born in 1995, I grew up with technology. I progressed, it progressed. In 10 years my progress will reach a grinding halt as I approach my thirties, technology may stay on pace with me. These are important times and history more than anything will evaluate the early use of the internet and its effect on society.

Relating pornography, bullying, hate speech, the dark web, dank memes, fake news, eBay, Vine, shopping online, trying to find, we dig through screens to find what we need and let our fake worlds impede on what life really means. A constant distraction that has left more data and information then you could ever sift through. They'll evaluate our attention spans, rises in mental illness, suicide, addiction, rape, rises in crime, Tinder and dating, socioeconomic shifts by race before and after the internet, the intimacy, the rise of irony, the insane nature of the blurred reality that we live in.

What's the biggest critique of reality television?

It's bullshit.

We can all put ourselves in the shoes of the cast of the Jersey Shore and see that they are playing to the cameras. There is a hint of reality, but there are huge lights, cameramen, and the knowledge that human beings will see what they are doing. Now compare that to Snapchat, Twitter, and Facebook. Everywhere you go, you have the potential to be recorded. Think of the thousands of pictures on your phone, the thousands of strangers in the background whom you accidentally have saved in pictures of yourself and your friends, and the thousands of pictures, videos, and hours of security camera footage that you've been in.

This all alters our behavior and the way we live our lives; how would you act if no one's phone had a camera? How would you dress? Who would you be? No Instagram, who are you? Are you really fashionable and trendy? Or did you copy and paste what is trending? Because companies decide what gets on those blogs, what celebrities wear, and the products for your hair, so what choices have you actually made? The same goes for men, in joggers, dressed like Justin Bieber, too focused on their daily fashion show to let their ambitions grow. It's time to let some of this shit go and be a little more careful.

That's where technology gets sad. We are **If & When** our "If" was "If technology advances how will people start to live their lives?" and the "When" was now. I'm not a "Millennial" I'm a part of the Beta Test Generation, the first to have phones as children, the first to have the freedom of the internet, the first to Uber to a keg, the first to broadcast themselves delivering Pizza Hut, I saw the dark web before I could drive a car. This world is absurd.

If you were born between 1989 and 1998, you were the world's guinea pig. Handed a Game Boy while your brain was in its formative stage, handed a phone "just to call mom if you're not safe", logging onto AIM, finding the games on your phone, your friends had Sidekicks, RZR's, Juke's, and then the enV Touch; then right as puberty approached... iPhone. How fitting.

That's just the beginning, the advertisements, larger than life films, porn, dating apps, porn, video game communities, friends who have never seen each other's faces, the failure of online education, and did I mention all of the goddamn pornography? Who would I be in 1960? We weren't given a chance to develop. I have no idea who I am.

That's why there are these problems, my options were Gatorade and cartoons, of course, I have ADHD. I've been seeing people get murdered on the internet since I was 12, of course, I'm going to be depressed. I've been handed all the information of the universe in a 20-minute video, of course, I'll lose my faith.

I watched Cartman, and Dave Chappelle adopted irony too young. Teachers told me I was dumb. I'd walk around basketball camp in prescription sports goggles screaming "I'm Rick James Bitch!"

Weapons of Mass Destruction, Corruption, the Gulf of Tonkin, organized slave trade, videos of Richard Nixon admitting he targeted "hippies and blacks" with drug laws, why would I have faith in a young country that's done so much wrong?

As I said, I didn't choose to be how I am. I was born in Philadelphia in 1995, I love cheesesteaks, and I'm not concerned about the opinions of anyone who doesn't care about me. Why?

Because this is all we will ever have, worrying about the past will only stunt you and worrying about other people's opinions when anyone can show up on your phone at any time is a dangerous precedent to set.

In no way am I blaming the issues my generation and humanity faces on technology and labeling technology as bad, this is just the way life works. People impose their will on the world, and it generates these insane side effects. Some brilliant people created a Gameboy, do you know how amazing that is? To make the first Gameboy. The side effects were barely even a thought, but Moore's Law carried the Gameboy into a Nintendo Switch, which I've never used but looks amazing. The development of technology as a whole will benefit more than it harms unless we end in a fiery nuclear holocaust, which is always an option. Death is always looming.

Of all the negativity that may have been portrayed throughout this book, there is one saving grace in humanity. We are very silly. There are behaviors and actions that are so downright random and unpredictable that they make life worth living. Contrary to the tone I've taken in this book, I love dancing. I think it's the dumbest fucking thing on the planet, but I love it.

Set this book down and start dancing where you are.

I'd guess that 2% of readers did it, but seriously, much like the metaphor in Chapter One, drawing parallels to the context of the national anthem, dancing is all context. You can't dance during a funeral service, but if you dance particularly well in a nightclub, it might lead to a relationship. The simple structure of dancing is so commonplace, that's why there's a "dance floor" for an act that is supposedly supposed to be "free flowing" and devoid of structure.

The stupidity of people amazes me, that's why I love the carnival. It's beautiful, the whole sentiment. Carnivals are composed of people with very little money, providing fun and entertainment to other people with very little money. No one gets anything done at a carnival. The only people that are stressed out at carnivals are white trash moms.

A carnival sliding board may be the most innocent invention of all time. Swirls painted down the side of a huge structure, built only to have humans climb up to go down. Who gets sad on a sliding board? It's not dangerous, costly, political; it's gender neutral, it is what it is, no bullshit. You go up, excited; then come down pleased. No context. Clean stupid fun.

It's not just dancing; it's alcohol, parties, Santa, Christmas, sports, music, cheese fries, all of that. The deeper the delusions go, the more fun they are. Santa Claus could be considered a legitimate case of mass hysteria in America. Lying to children with the prospect of building hope in something wonderful, but a harmless little lie that will later help them challenge other fallacies in the future.

These stupid and silly behaviors are ultimately the best parts of life. Love skiing? Think about how stupid it is to strap yourself to wooden planks and fall down a frozen mountain. I love basketball. It's just people throwing a ball into a circle, glorified throwing garbage into a can. Yes, these things take intense skill and training, but consider the fact that we made all of this shit up.

I break everything down to its bare minimum and then evaluate. Dancing is just moving around. Music is just noise. These are just shapes on paper. You own the meaning, to everything, to all of this. It's all subjective, and no one else's opinions really matter. I wrote this, but don't even get to decide what it means to you. That's the power we all have. You owe nobody anything. You are owed nothing. Now in front of you, you have the rules to the game which are lenient and subjective, make the most of it. Whatever that means to you.

I've been thinking about what it is I want to do with my life.
But nothing seems to be right.
Not with me, the sciences, or the world; nothing is what it seems like.
The seams of the fabric of society often lie to me.
Privacy, scarce.
A public unaware.
Where do I find solace in a place so unpolished?

I've found solace in stupidity.
Trying to learn how to live for me.
I'm not happy, and I don't need to be.

Friends by my side,
no reasons to hide.
I enjoy being alive.

I'm done trying to be happy; I'm just going to live my life.
I'm done trying to do everything right.

So scared of honesty, my whole life, I've tried to hide it.
On Earth it's easy to feel small, I'll live the Life of a Giant.

Thank you.

TO ANYONE THAT PICKED THIS BOOK UP AND FINISHED IT.

Life doesn't just "have" a point or a purpose.
You have to give your life a purpose.

157

References and citations:

Evolutiontheorist. "Posts about Bell Curve on Evolutionistx."

Evolutionistx, 24 May 2016,

evolutionistx.wordpress.com/tag/bell-curve/.

Kaku, Michio. *Physics of the Future: How Science Will Shape*

Human Destiny and Our Daily Lives by the Year 2100. Anchor

Books, 2012.

Klosterman, Chuck. *But What If We're Wrong?: Thinking about the*

Present as If It Were the Past. Blue Rider Press, 2017.

Kwatz, Paul. *Conscious Robots: If We Really Had Free Will, What*

Would We Do All Day? Peacock's Tail Publishing, 2017.

McLeod, Saul. "Maslow's Hierarchy of Needs." *Simply*

Psychology, 4 Feb. 2016,

www.simplypsychology.org/maslow.html.

Staff, Investopedia. "Moore's Law." *Investopedia*, 24 Nov.

2003, www.investopedia.com/terms/m/mooreslaw.asp

Rogan, Joe, and Natasha Leggero. "Joe Rogan Experience." *Joe Rogan Experience*, Los Angeles, California, 7 June 2015. Podcast

wikiHow. "How to Diagram Sentences." *WikiHow*, WikiHow, 19 Oct. 2017, www.wikihow.com/Diagram-Sentences.

Made in the USA
Columbia, SC
08 January 2018